BE A
FREE
RANGE
HUMAN

Life can be much broader once you discover
one simple fact: everything around you
that you call life was made up by
people that were no smarter than you.
And you can change it, you can influence it,
you can build your own things...

The minute that you understand that you can
poke life, you can mould it... once you learn that,
you'll never be the same again.

Steve Jobs

BE A FREE RANGE HUMAN

ESCAPE THE 9 TO 5, CREATE A LIFE YOU LOVE AND STILL PAY THE BILLS

Marianne Cantwell

KoganPage

LONDON PHILADELPHIA NEW DELHI

First published in Great Britain and the United States in 2013 by Kogan Page Limited

120 Pentonville Road	1518 Walnut Street, Suite 1100	4737/23 Ansari Road
London N1 9JN	Philadelphia PA 19102	Daryaganj
United Kingdom	USA	New Delhi 110002
www.koganpage.com		India

© Marianne Cantwell, 2013

The right of Marianne Cantwell to be identified as the author of this work has been asserted by her in accordance with the Copyright, Designs and Patents Act 1988.

ISBN   978 0 7494 6610 7
E-ISBN 978 0 7494 6611 4

British Library Cataloguing-in-Publication Data

A CIP record for this book is available from the British Library.

Library of Congress Cataloging-in-Publication Data

Cantwell, Marianne.
    Be a free range human : escape the 9-5, create a life you love and still pay the bills / Marianne Cantwell.
        p. cm.
    ISBN 978-0-7494-6610-7 – ISBN 978-0-7494-6611-4   1. Career development.
2. Job satisfaction.   3. Self-employed.   4. Flextime.   I. Title.
    HF5381.C26155 2012
    650.1–dc23   2012026746

Typeset by Graphicraft Limited, Hong Kong
Print production managed by Jellyfish
Printed and bound by CPI Group (UK) Ltd, Croydon, CR0 4YY

PRAISE FOR
BE A FREE RANGE HUMAN

*A practical guidebook loaded with exactly the tools you need to
break free of excuses and start creating the adventurous life of
your dreams. Marianne Cantwell knows what she's talking about.
Pay attention.*
Barbara J Winter, author, *Making a Living Without a Job*

*Imaginative, inspirational, and challenging. A unique, well-written
book that will have a huge impact on readers.*
**Dr Barrie Hopson, author of 40 books including
Build Your Own Rainbow and *And What Do You Do?*
*10 Steps To Creating A Portfolio Career***

*This book will give you the encouragement and practical advice
you need to embark on a whole new freer way of life. Whether
you are feeling trapped by your current job, or the drudgery of
daily life, read this and realize that the world is your oyster. With
just a few quid, you really can change your life. Marianne will
show you how to work smarter and make all the money you need
to do what you want with your life, whether that's hanging with
your kids, lying on a beach or living in a cave!*

*If self-help books make you cringe and business books bore you
to tears, try something a whole lot smarter instead. This is realistic
and do-able. No long winded business plans or seed capital
required; just you, your ambitions and this book. Marianne is
funny, frank and feisty and she really knows her stuff. This is the
kind of book you'll take everywhere with you – it'll be your new
best buddy, supporting and encouraging you on the road to living
la vida free range-a!*
Nadia Finer, author, *More to Life than Shoes*

*Be a Free Range Human shines. This book could have stopped at
merely inspiring millions of frustrated cubicle-dwellers to think
outside the job box. Thankfully Cantwell goes the extra mile to
not only give the 'what' and the 'why' of crafting a life of purpose
and freedom, but to provide the reader with the all-important*

'how'. *Changing course is never easy. But as* Be a Free Range Human *reminds us, it is most definitely worth it.*

Valerie Young, Founder and Dreamer in Residence at ChangingCourse.com since 1995. Author of *The Secret Thoughts of Successful Women*

This is one of the most useful guides I've read – and I've read a lot – to help you create a realistic (read: totally do-able) life you want to live; it is also fun to read. Each chapter is packed with insightful exercises, checklists and tips, as well as a multitude of examples and case studies to prove that you are not mad to want a free range lifestyle. If I hadn't already made the leap myself, this would be the book I'd use.

Lea Woodward, entrepreneur and founder of LocationIndependent.com

Need and want are two very different things. Many of us get stuck in jobs we need to do – to pay the bills – rather than the jobs we want to do. Jumping from one to the other is scary. It's like jumping a river full of crocodiles. But it can be done. It may mean a few sacrifices – you soon learn what you need, rather than what you want – but the rewards are worth it. I was a police officer, which I enjoyed. Now I'm a writer and artist, which I love. All it took was passion, confidence and a little planning. I got there on my own but if I'd had this wise and clever book at the time, it would have helped me immensely. If, for no other reason than because I could have used it to swat the crocodiles.

Stevyn Colgan, author, artist, QI 'elf' and co-writer of BBC Radio 4's *The Museum of Curiosity*

Reading Marianne Cantwell's guide to escaping the cage of modern life is like sitting down for a one-to-one with the best sort of best friend – the one who helps you work through your ideas, suggests solutions, and, best of all, always believes in you. If you've ever wondered what life's like outside the cage, buy this book – and you too could become a Free Range Human.

James Wallman, The Future Laboratory

CONTENTS

PART 4 BUILD YOUR FREE RANGE ESCAPE HATCH 147

Get started, get known fast, and start earning that free range income (even while still in your job!). An unconventional guide on how to build things up, stand out from the crowd, and then escape the career-cage trap in your 10 steps to freedom. Discover how to earn the income, get the lifestyle and break free (on your terms).

You're not building a business,
you're creating a life.
And that starts now.

ACKNOWLEDGEMENTS

Liz Gooster: you found me, met me, and birthed the book with me. Thank you for believing in this project and its author. I hope your own travel adventures continue!

Robert Watson: in editing this book, you took an ENFP's enthusiastic mess and INTJd it into what it is today. Thank you for taking on the two week deadline: Novocastrians can pull off anything!

Dad: thank you for your patience with a daughter who threw away several 'good careers'. I'm amazed at how much you've taken to free range ideas after years of 'not really knowing what my daughter does for a living'. I hope you enjoy this book.

The old 'brain trust': John Williams and Selina Barker. Oh my. Look at how far we have come from our meetings in the Hub! I will always be grateful for the two years the three of us spent in close collaboration and what we gave one another. As with everything each of us began in that period, this book would not be the same without you. Thank you for going above and beyond: John for being there in the first months (listening patiently to my long monologues and gently pointing out how to actually write a book); Selina for being there in that last month (and encouraging me to keep my voice in here: you were right).

Barbara Winter: you were the first to reply when I had the idea for this book. 'I was wondering when a book deal was coming your way', you said – which instantly made me feel this wasn't a nutty idea after all. Thanks for the emergency cross-Atlantic Skype calls. I stand by my comment that you are the grandmother of the industry!

Manar Hussain: often the words 'this book wouldn't exist without you' sound like an exaggeration. In this case, they are not. Were it not for an unlikely coincidence involving mixed-up mail, Olympic hockey tickets and your ability to ask 'why' continuously, then this book would not exist today. Many hugs.

Dave Brown and Jenny Jameson: you got this book kicked off by reading and categorizing years of my writing – a brave task! Jenny, knowing you've got my back has kept me sane more than once, thank you. Dave, thanks for your Sydney hospitality (I hope your Country Club forgave the 'unauthorized guest' situation. Darn Beige Army).

Barrie Hopson: thanks for the encouragement and 'out of the box' plotting over tea! Can't wait to read your 40th book.

James Wallman: after weeks of agonizing over the introduction, one hour with you in Leon had it sorted. Amazing. Hurry up and get your book out there!

The Free Range Tribe: Much love and gratitude to everyone who has replied to my Friday 'love letters' on the Free Range Humans email list over the years. In generously sharing your stories, dreams and fears you have shaped this book more than you know. Thanks to the amazing group of regular commenters on the Free Range Humans Facebook fan page including Soozi, Rachel, Liz, Julia, Vicky, Natasha, Laura, Lucinda, Dan, Gemma, Michelle, Katie, Caroline, Stephanos, and Lucy (among many others). Other 'fledglings' who contributed their experiences and guinea pigged exercises: Dominic, Jay, Maria, Sally, Susan, Scott, Tim, Ruth, and Wendy (extra thanks to Natasha Blackman for suggesting the Dos and Don'ts, and Hattie Brazely for contributing to the Beige Army's voice).

Friends who welcomed me into their homes at various points on my writer-y travels: Shirley Morgan, Heather Martin, Claire Noonan, Debbie Masters, Emma Reynolds, Cherie Todd and Andrew Whalan. Special thanks to Kim Willis for feedback about the first draft (and for being excellent at brainstorming even when tired). And thanks to Max the Dog for his inspiring barking.

Finally, the places where this book was written: Brick Lane Coffee House, Flat White, Allpress, Emporium Bakery, Gallery Café, and Pavilion Café (London); Frankie's (Newcastle, Australia); Riverbend Books Teahouse (Brisbane); Gertrude & Alice and Chapter One (Sydney); Fattoria Bassetto in Tuscany, and all the wonderful people at Shanti Lodge, Phuket where I holed up for a month to complete this book (your teeny kittens made my stay).

PROLOGUE

Alarm rings. Get up. Feed cat. Late to work. Walk up the hill and down into the tube station. This is all I'll see of the outside world all day.

Every morning the same commute, packed in a tube train so closely that all I can see and smell is the next person's armpit.

Standing there I look at the people around me. We are supposed to be some of the most successful humans of our generation and we are sleep deprived, stressed and packed into a metal box on our way to an office-shaped box. Someone isn't wearing deodorant. The guy next to me, in the Hugo Boss suit, is listening to dance music on his iPod, pretending to be alive for just one moment.

The doors open and more people cram in so that every part of my body is touching someone else's. I can't breathe.

Someone steps on my foot and I can't move out of the way. If we were animals this would not be legal. Battery cage humans going from our commute cage to our career cage, when all I want to do is run out of there, past the buildings and roam free in the sunshine. The thought strikes me 'I want to be a free range human'.

Then someone's elbow strikes me and I forget all about that crazy dream.

For now.

INTRODUCTION

From beach to boardroom

'Enjoy your adventures now,' said my Dad, 'you won't be able to do that sort of thing when you...'

And just then the line went. I was on a payphone – remember those? – in Koh Samui. I was 22. Feet in the sand, flip-flops in my hand and a queue of bedraggled Full Moon backpackers outside, waiting to make their calls. This was the first time I'd talked to Dad for a month, and I'd just told him I was going trekking in the jungle.

'Can't hear you, Dad...'

'I said...' he shouted through the bad line '... you won't be able to do that sort of thing when you grow up and get a proper job.'

Did anyone ever tell you the same thing? After all, that's how life is supposed to be, isn't it? Have fun, then settle down, commute, work, commute, die (with a few years at the end, if you're lucky).

Dreams aren't meant to last. They're what you have when you're young and foolish. They're what you give up when you get a real job. *Everyone knows that.*

Everyone except, it seemed, the 22-year-old me. Standing in the sunshine, phone in hand, I just laughed. Why would I do that? This was wonderful. I couldn't see anything that would make me give up this life of freedom!

Fast-forward a few years later and I was firmly seconded in a corporate job. Sitting at my desk, I adjusted my Prada glasses, pushed aside my sandwich and sighed at yet another spreadsheet. There was no question of ending up on a tropical island *that* afternoon.

In fact, from my cubicle in the head office of a multinational company, located smack bang in the middle of a busy London roundabout, there was little chance of ending up anywhere that wasn't surrounded by concrete, cars and buildings all day long.

The worst part? It wasn't the spreadsheet. It wasn't the way I seemed to get every cold that was going around. It wasn't even that people kept telling me I was lucky to have such a 'great job'... while I secretly felt I was dying inside. The worst part wasn't any of that.

The worst part was the attitude. Everyone around me seemed to think this was normal – they seemed resigned to this career-cage fate. 'I had such adventures when I was younger,' reminisced an older colleague. 'I wish I could do that sort of thing now. Of course you have to get it out of your system before reality strikes.'

What? *Reality?* This man thought that this life – in an artificially built, over-air conditioned building in the middle of a screaming roundabout, hardly seeing daylight three months of the year, with the only hope of escape being winning the lottery – he thought that was *reality?*

Somewhere, somehow, things had gone terribly wrong.

Then again, what did I know? Maybe this man was right. Maybe I should just grow up and accept that this was real life. So that's what I did. From that moment on, I threw myself into my career. Rose the ranks. Ended up at director level in a City consultancy at a relatively young age.

Yet, still something was missing. On the last day of every holiday, fuelled by weeks of freedom and sunshine, I'd promise that *this* would be the time I'd finally figure out what I really wanted to do with my life and get out of there. But within days of getting back to the office, that promise would be forgotten.

One day a friend shared the story of someone who had packed in her job for a dream life, and we all thought it was fabulous. We all said we'd do it too... well, you know... one day. You could tell that 'one day' wasn't exactly scheduled into the diary.

I mean, come on. Those escapes are for someone younger and freer, someone older and richer, someone with a different CV. Nice dream, but I wasn't 22 any more. I had bills to pay. A career to consider. *Someone like me doesn't do something like that.*

We have been brought up to believe that a job is your only sensible option. But is it?

What I do now (work or pleasure?)

Last Tuesday, I boarded a train from Milan to Florence, backpack in one hand and laptop in the other. I took the seat next to a nice American woman who smiled, glanced at my laptop and asked the inevitable: *'Are you travelling for business or pleasure?'*

That question always trips me up. Work or play? I'm not sure. I'm here for a month, my entire business is in my backpack, and yes I'm going to work but it's work I could do anywhere in the world. Plus, I'm going to explore and enjoy the country (ie eat unfeasible amounts of pasta and say 'ciao' to cute boys serving espressos). Anyway, I'm not sure where the line between 'work' and 'play' ends any more because I love what I do for a living.

All of which may have been too much information for a smiling stranger on the 9.35 train to Florence. So I gave the easy answer: 'I'm going to Tuscany to write a book.'

True. However, between you and me, there's a better answer. That answer is the reason I'm writing this book for you. The best way to put it is: *I am a Free Range Human.*

Jobs are so last century (welcome to free ranging)

That career advice you got at school all those years ago is out of date. More and more people are saying no thanks to the conventional job and are busting out of their beige offices to create remarkable lives, on their own terms.

The mission? Freedom and fulfilment: not in retirement, not in their annual vacation, but every single day, starting now. These people are the new Free Range Humans.

Free Range Humans work when, where and how they want and get paid to do what they love. Today you can find Free Range Humans all around the world working happily with their laptops from parks, cafés, beaches and their kitchen tables, making a great living without an office or a boss:

★ Some free rangers use their new-found independence to travel the world full time, such as Hannah and Chris who left office life to help companies hire better talent... while on their laptops on the other side of the world.

★ Others stay at home and spend time with their families, such as Emma who left her job as a marketing-campaign manager to make a full-time living from YouTube videos... and watch her kids grow up.

★ Others take the opportunity to pack everything they love into a portfolio career so that they don't have to settle on choosing just one thing, such as Elisavet who quit her job as a BBC producer and now creates popular cookery courses and gets paid to write about music.

★ Others use the free range approach to break into their dream field, without having to convince an employer to hire them as a career changer, such as Charlie who went from regular office bod to running amazing urban writers' retreats.

★ And, of course, others create a life that allows them to make an income while offline, unplugged and lying in a hammock with a mojito (that would be me, then).

The free range tribe isn't united by travel or a particular industry: this growing tribe is united in taking a unique approach to problem solving and income creation that gives you the freedom to get paid to do whatever you darn well please and create an amazing lifestyle in the process.

Sounds completely crazy? I agree: a few years ago, making a living without a proper job was a crazy far-off dream that only a 'lucky' few achieved, but now things are different. Most people don't know about this new option but those who do are poking their heads out of the career cage, blinking in the sunlight and flapping their wings to a better, free range life. You can too (and this book shows you how).

Why this is possible now

We are living at a remarkable point in history. Right now, you can make a living from pretty much anything you can imagine. In the last five to ten years alone, technology has zoomed forward beyond anything your college career adviser thought possible and beyond anything you read in the job ads:

★ Today, you can run a global seminar without even getting out of bed.

★ You can pack your entire business in your backpack and take off around the world (while still seeing money drop into your bank account).

★ You can reach 1,000 people at once and create a consistent income in a way that was unimaginable 20 years ago.

★ You can get known fast, without going to a single early morning networking meeting.

★ You can have an idea, draw it out, and launch in under two weeks...

Crucially, you can do this right now without even quitting your job. Starting this evening – from the comfort of your kitchen table – you can experiment, run a 'prototype project', and start with the ideas in this book *before* deciding to say goodbye to the boss. This is how I quit my last ever job and how hundreds of other free rangers do it too. (Of course if you have to leave your job right now, we have options to help with that too!)

Never before has it been possible to go from idea to income so easily, but most people still don't know how to make this work (I certainly didn't when I was in my career cage). Here's why:

The gap between assumptions and reality

Recently, I went on a boat trip to some beautiful islands in southern Thailand. Clear blue waters, cavorting monkeys on islands and endless snorkelling. On the boat I met lovely people, most of whom had jobs back in the 'real world'. They spoke of how they would love to stay here forever instead of going back to the office at the end of their holiday. Over the course of the day one person made three comments that stuck in my mind. These comments contain common assumptions about work – see if you can identify them:

1 *About herself*: 'I guess the good thing about working in the corporate world is that you can afford to visit beautiful places like this.'

2 *About the boat captain*: 'He must be doing well. That's the life. Move to Thailand and get rich off a boat company. Maybe he can hire me!'

3 *About me*: 'Being able to write and travel must be nice. Do you work in pubs or something to keep going?'

Did you identify the assumptions?

Assumption 1   You have to work in a job to get to visit beautiful places and have a great lifestyle. I hadn't yet told them that I had been hanging out there for four months and hadn't set foot in an office for years.

Assumption 2   Big shiny infrastructure – especially expensive stuff like boats – automatically means a great income. Truth? I spoke to the captain and he confided that even though his tours sell out almost every day, he barely breaks even. The costs simply don't work – the boat makes him look 'rich' but the fuel and the staff don't come free. (So no, he isn't going to hire her).

Assumption 3   If you don't have a job and don't have a business that revolves around something you can touch (such as boats) then you're little better than unemployed. You must be broke. That's the killer assumption, and that's what we are going to challenge throughout this book.

What I am going to show you is how to figure out what you want, create a life that suits you down to the ground, and build a great income doing it. The strategies you will learn do not involve owning boats, but they do give you the freedom to hang about diving off them as much as you like.

Welcome to the Third Way

Free ranging is the Third Way between jobs and high-risk entrepreneurship. This is a new game, with new rules. No funding, no big risky investment, no premises, no staff, but bags of personality, play and freedom: that's a free range business. I'm going to show you simple ways to start with what you have and how to create a free range income that *more than replicates your monthly pay cheque* (but gives you way more freedom and fulfilment than a job).

This book shows that you have options other than staying in a job for the rest of your days. Which rather begs the question:

What do you really want to do with your life?

I'm betting that at least once in the last year you have tried to figure out your 'dream job'. I'm also betting you haven't *quite* settled on one answer yet.

Here's how it usually works: you struggle for years to identify one perfect job. After much searching, maybe you find it, fantastic! You've discovered your dream career! Now, you better hope you're qualified for it, hope it pays enough, and hope the employer agrees to take you on. If you get past those hurdles (which most don't) the next step is to squeeze the entirety of your rich, complex personality and dreams into that one tiny job description and give up on the bits that don't fit. Then, you had better hope you'll still love it five years down the line because you don't want to go through all *that* again.

Tra la. Your dream job. Congratulations.

Doesn't that sound less than ideal to you?

The truth is that you are way more interesting and complex than a single job description. As a Free Range Human you get to *create* your own dream career when no one job ticks the boxes. You decide where you spend your days, what you do, and how you do it. You can combine several interests tailored to suit your unique personality. No more packing yourself into a box.

If you want to do something very different to what you do now, there's a bonus: free range career change is easier than changing fields in the job world. You don't have to convince an employer to take you on and you don't need a perfectly matching CV. A Free Range Human can build status in a new field quickly, make the move to pretty much anything that takes their fancy, and constantly evolve that as they grow and change.

In this book you are not going to search aimlessly for your dream solution, you are going to learn how to grab the reins and *create* it. The pay off? Your life, lived in full colour every day.

You can join us

The free range tribe is growing and we'd love you to join us. This isn't a pipe dream reserved for the 'lucky ones'. More and more people are discovering that life no longer has to be a choice between trapped and well-off versus free and broke. I am going to lift the lid and show you how real career-cage escapes happen and how you can do it too.

What you will discover

In this book you will learn:

- ★ How to figure out what you really want to do with your life (and how to create your own bespoke 'dream career').

- ★ How to tweak any idea to suit your personality so you don't have to squeeze yourself into another box.

- ★ How to get paid *more* by being more you.

- ★ How to make this happen *without* an idea for a world-changing widget.

- ★ How to test an idea and get going without even quitting your job.

- ★ How to go from zero to 'go-to' person in your industry in months.

- ★ How to start for under £100, with no funding (ie no debt), and get your first project out there in two weeks.

★ How to stand out from the crowd and get paid what you deserve.

★ How to fast-track your journey to get better results in six months than many old-style businesses achieve in six years.

★ More to the point, you will learn how to create a lifestyle you truly love... while earning a consistent income that more than pays the bills.

In the first half of this book (Parts 1 and 2), you'll figure out what you want. Then, in Parts 3 and 4 you'll start to hatch your escape plan.

What this book is not

Before you think that I'm going to paint some crazy vision of quitting your job, finding some dodgy 'money making scheme' and hanging out all year doing nothing except working on your tan, let's get real here.

1 **This isn't a get rich quick book.** I haven't found some easy button you can press – and neither have the successful Free Range Humans I know. In fact, if someone offers you an 'overnight get rich quick scheme', run the other way: in my research I've found that overnight success happens after many nights of getting off your butt and *making stuff happen.*

   The trick is making the right stuff happen so you can enjoy your life. When you know what works (and what doesn't) you can ditch 90 per cent of the activities that people unknowingly waste time on in their first year, and focus only on the 10 per cent that really matters. Those fast-track strategies you will learn in this book.

2 **This isn't a conventional business or careers book.** Screw risking it all for the teeny chance of a pay-off down the line. This is a book about you: doing what you love and living the life you want to live *right freaking now*.

In this book you'll be putting your strengths, your personality and your dreams smack bang at the centre of every decision you make, so you can create a really-right lifestyle for yourself. To get it right, we will spend time upfront getting crystal clear on what you really want to do and creating your own solution that fits you perfectly.

This book is written as though I were sitting across from you, looking you in the eye, and telling you, as a friend, what you need to do to get free. I don't care if the critics say this book is too colloquial or informal. *I didn't write it for them, I wrote it for you.* No BS. The occasional strong language. Why? So that you *get* this on an emotional as well as an intellectual level. Business-speak sometimes sanitizes important ideas so you go away thinking, 'Oh yeah, I suppose I should do that... one day.' Screw that. This is about your life: a darn important topic (the most important one of all IMHO), and if it takes the *occasional enthusiastic italic* to make a point, so be it.

3 **This isn't a book about travel.** Yes, some free rangers use their new-found freedom to travel, but it's not mandatory! In fact, at least half the people profiled in this book have little interest in travelling. This book doesn't tell you to live any particular lifestyle, it empowers you to create the life you want, whatever that may be. (However if you are interested in travel, Chapter 31 shows you how to create that lifestyle).

4 **This isn't for someone else (it is for you).** This isn't about 'luck' or a clever idea. This isn't 'alright for her but not for the likes of me'. This isn't for someone with a different looking CV and no bills to pay.

This is for *you*, honey. I know you picked up this book for a reason. You want something more than what you have now and that's not going to come from wishing, waiting or browsing another set of job ads.

Free range is the new career change. And it's far smarter than waiting for retirement, wasting your one and only life settling for second best.

Right now, thousands of people just like you are realizing that the answer to 'what do I really want to do with my life' and 'how do I get to get paid to have fun' are much closer than you think. Odds are you've been thinking about this for a while, going around in circles trying to find the solution. This is where that cycle ends. Today, we start your journey from career-cage employee to Free Range Human.

Who am I to write this book?

Two answers:

1. I'm someone who has done it for real

A few years ago I was where you are now. Book in hand, trying to figure out what to do (and how to get paid for it). Soon after that phone call with my Dad, I fell into a corporate career working with companies such as Disney – until I woke up one day, years older, knowing I desperately wanted out... but with no idea where to turn.

Long story short, everything changed when I stopped furtively browsing the job ads looking for that dream job, and invested the time in discovering how to create my own career instead. I built up my business on the side... and then quit my job to launch as a newbie in a crowded field, in the middle of a recession.

Yet by the end of my first year I was earning *more* per month in my free range life than I ever had in that 'good job' (you know, the one I hung on to for fear of going broke). In this book you will learn the techniques I used to make that happen.

Today, I'm living the free range life for real. Because travel is important to me, I run my free range career around the world (this book was written in five different countries). And that's all fun.

But what I love most is the work I do. And that's the main reason I'm writing this book.

2. I've helped thousands of others do it too

When I quit my job I had no intention of showing others how to go free range. But after I broke free, people would take me to one side and whisper: '*How did you get out? Can you help me do it too?*' So, one rainy afternoon, I started a little blog called Free Range Humans. It grew into my main vocation today.

Today, I help people discover what they *really* want to do, then help them quit their jobs to create amazing lives in which they get paid to be themselves. To do this, I run Free Range Humans courses online, speak around the world, and do a happy dance each time I receive an email from a client who has broken free (you will see their stories throughout this book).

This book is informed by years of helping people discover and live their own adventures, whatever they may be. So, while I opened up with my story, this isn't a book about me. It's a book about what really works to discover your dreams and turn them into a (paying) reality.

This is the book I wished I had when I was back in my job. Use it well.

How to read this book

Do the damn exercises

If you're as impatient as I am, it is tempting to skim through looking for an answer. However you can't get the answers just from reading. Real insights come in doing, not in 'thinking about it'. You are worth the extra five minutes it takes to do an exercise, so get that pen ready.

TIP Watch out for those 'I already know all about *that*' moments: in my experience of working with clients, the exercises that feel most uncomfortable are probably the ones that you most need to do.

Take the reins

This book is intended to be read from start to finish and that is how I suggest you approach it for the best results. However, feel free to ignore this advice. Want to skip ahead? Do it. This is your journey, do it in whatever way will work best for you: that's the free range approach and it applies to everything you do from now on.

Think like a Free Range Human

Don't look for the perfect example of someone exactly in your situation who made the exact move you are thinking of making. You simply won't find them: look hard enough and there will *always* be a reason why someone's situation was different, and always a reason why it might not be possible. The question is, are you going to choose to let that stop you?

Remember, no one who made their escape is any better than you. Free rangers are not smarter, richer, younger, older or more attractive; they don't have a certain CV and their situation is not down to fate. Fate is what happens when you get up and do things other people thought they could only achieve when 'luck' came knocking.

My journey from stressed career-cage worker to Free Range Human was not about luck or connections, it was down to thinking like a free ranger and learning about this new world's possibilities. Possibilities, that, back then, I didn't even know were out there. In this book, you're going to discover them too. We are going to explore, have fun and bust you out of there.

PART 1
GET READY FOR THE
RIDE

1 WHAT YOUR SCHOOL CAREER ADVISER NEVER TOLD YOU

The 'safe job' myth

I need to pay the bills therefore I need to keep my job. It's fine to dream but you have to get back to reality.

As one stuck career cager said: 'When I start thinking about making the change, what goes through my head is a whole heap of reasons not to jump – we need a steady income, what happens if it goes wrong and I can't pay the bills?'

If you want to provide for your family (or your cat), and not end up homeless in a cardboard box, then reality says to stay put.

Myth buster

Up until recently, most people made a deal: 'I'll work (in a job I don't necessarily love) in return for a salary I can rely on.' The aim was a job for life: work all day and then play on weekends and in retirement.

But then, work hours started getting longer and jobs stopped being safe. Look at your employment contract right now: what's your notice period? One month? Three months? That's exactly how much security you have. Don't kid yourself that you have permanence.

Of course, the job-for-life generation also told us that if we worked hard we'd end up with a great retirement. If we stuck at that soul-sapping job, when we were 60 we could live fabulously, travel and have a whale of a time (assuming you make it that far).

Wait a minute… would those be with those same retirement plans that went down the tube in the crash of 2008? Where thousands upon thousands of regular people who had worked their whole life for the dream at the end were left stranded?

Analysts are predicting that a large percentage of the population won't be able to retire until their seventies or eighties.[1] A long time to wait. *That career-cage deal isn't looking so hot now.* This is the new reality of the workplace. The question is: are you still playing by the old rules?

The old rules

Jobs have not always been the default way to make a living. Prior to the Industrial Revolution in the late 1800s, working for yourself was seen as a normal and laudable pursuit. However, when factories emerged, priorities changed. Factories needed compliant workers to follow the rules. Soon, innovation, individuality and creative thinking were no longer seen as valuable skills for the majority of the population.

That's how we created our career-cage workers all those years ago: cogs in a factory, and then the factory became an office. *Do your job, don't ask questions. Work isn't something you're meant to enjoy.* We were taught to be competent, comply and you'll have a good career.

Then, all of a sudden, the old rules stopped working.

Jobs started to be automated. Today, a computer can do the work of a dozen people in roles as varied as data entry, engineering and even law. As that change shook the world, the Internet came along and globalization took off. Jobs across previously untouchable industries were being farmed out to India, China and whoever would do it the cheapest. Then, in the economic crash of 2008, many of the jobs that were left were consolidated; I bet you know at least one person who is now covering the workload previously shouldered by two people.

Suddenly, the game changed. And the myth of the safe job changed with it.

Jobs are a stupid idea in this economy

Here's why:

1 **Jobs are risky.** With job security out the window for most people, employment is the equivalent to being self-employed with *only one client* (your employer). And as any business expert will tell you, being 100 per cent dependent on one client, in a turbulent market, is a very risky business. If they get into trouble, there goes your income.

2 **Someone else is in control of your life.** As an employee, the reality is that you have little control over the source of your income. Call me crazy, but I don't want someone else to determine whether I get my next pay cheque or end up on the streets.

   I notice that many of my friends in jobs are afraid of the economy and nervous about what 'the board' is going to decide next. In contrast, my free range friends see any change as an opportunity (indeed many of the greatest companies in the world were created by entrepreneurs who seized the moment in recessions[2]).

   You see, this is not about escaping a job once. It's about the freedom that comes when you know how to make money on your own terms. True freedom is being able to dance with the changes rather than being a victim to your circumstances.

3 **Jobs suck.** When you work a job, someone else has control of what you do, when you work, what you earn, what you work on, and when you are allowed to take a day off. You abdicate choice over what you do every day for most of your life in exchange for a pay cheque. This is the 'employment compromise'.

   With jobs less secure than ever and free range incomes easier to create than any other time in history, does this compromise really make sense?[3]

While everyone around you simultaneously complains about their job and is terrified of losing it, here's how to get free and get happy. **What a free range business looks like:**

- ★ no funding or debt needed;
- ★ start now for under £100;
- ★ no expensive premises needed to get started;
- ★ based on your personality, your passions and the life you want;
- ★ playful, flexible and able to change as you do.

Perfect for right now: cheap to start, super profitable and able to be moulded around you. The truth is that there is no reason why you have to work for someone else if you don't want to. Fabulous adventures and a lifetime of discovery awaits outside that office door.

Wait, don't the majority of small businesses fail?

This is the showstopper. You get all excited about the possibilities... and then you hear this. *Splat.* With that one line any dreams of breaking free are dashed. Problem is, that 'fact' simply is not true. Duncan Bannatyne, serial entrepreneur and star of the UK's *Dragons' Den*, points out that:

> *A lot of people don't want to have to face family and friends who were always sceptical of their chances of success. They've probably heard the statistic that 50 per cent of businesses fail in their first two years, but this statistic is usually based on the closure of business bank accounts NOT the close of businesses.*
>
> *If you remove the number of businesses that change bank accounts when introductory deals run out, or the number of businesses that are wound up because the founder took up a lucrative job offer, or started another business, the so-called failure rate drops dramatically.*
>
> *Barclays New Business Division estimates that the number of businesses that close because of 'external financial stress' ie owing money, is just 12 per cent in the first year.*[4]

Saying that a business failed because someone moved on is like saying anyone who quit their job and moved on to another one 'failed' at that job (even if they left to take a promotion). Ridiculous right?

Yes, of course some businesses do 'fail' in the conventional sense – but between you and me, one look at their website and approaches usually makes it pretty clear why. This is not about random luck. There are specific things to do to ensure this works. We are going to explore those in the second half of the book (and remember, with a free range business you are not sinking in loads of money and putting your house on the line! You're starting small – you can even get going while still in your job – and playing it out to create a tailor-made career that you love, and that more than pays the bills). For now consider this:

Free range third way

The question is: do you want to *feel* secure, or *be* secure?

The reality is that neither option, job or free range, is ever going to be 100 per cent secure. No option ever is. What matters is: when change happens (and it will) are you positioned as a potential victim or a potential winner?

There is an irony here. A job feels secure while a business does not. It feels secure to get a pay cheque – and those big glass buildings look to be so real and solid. *But the reality is that going free range gives you that sort of lifetime security that an employee imagines they have – until the moment they realize they really, really don't.*

Put that way, ask yourself again: 'Can I afford to escape the 9–5?' This time also ask yourself: 'Can I afford not to?'

2 WHY THIS MATTERS NOW

Three weeks after I left my teens, my mum died from cancer. Yes, I still miss her, and no it doesn't get any easier.

Her passing left me with a strong awareness of the shortness of life. Across the top of my laptop are the words: *'One life, baby. One life'*. Every morning I look at those words and remember the real stakes here.

What would you do if you had only one life?

(You do, you know.)

If you get one thing from this book, get this: stop kidding yourself that you have 300 years to live. 'Someday' is code for never; 'one day' is the path for taking your dreams to the grave with you.

There will never be a 'right time' to make the change. Everyone thinks they are too old or too young, too poor or too well paid, too attached or too single – and certainly too busy. The truth is that there never will be a perfect time, age or situation.

There are also no second chances.

Except the one you give yourself, starting today.

EXERCISE Part 1 reflections – where I am now

I picked up this book because: _____

_____

_____

Of what I have read so far, what resonated with me is: _____

_____

_____

▶

The things I don't enjoy about my current work-life are: _____

_____

_____

I have been dreaming of making a change for _____

_____ months/years

It is important for me to make a change because: _____

_____

The biggest question I have right now is: _____

_____

_____

Notes

1   Wu, Ke Bin, Family Income Sources for Older Persons, 2009, *AARP Public Policy Institute* http://assets.aarp.org/rgcenter/ppi/econ-sec/fs224-economic.pdf. See also an article entitled 'Budget 2012: Kids of today face working until they are 80 years old' published in *The Metro* (London), 21 March 2012, by John Higginson: http://www.metro.co.uk/news/893864-budget-2012-kids-of-today-face-working-until-they-are-80-years-old

2   Abrams, Rhonda. 'Strategies: It's a good time to start a business' published in *USA Today*, 17 October 2008

3   In fact, as political economist James Robertson points out, the free range way of working (which he calls ownwork) is a growing trend, 'key to the future of work and leisure' and the next step to break from 'the natural progression from slavery to serfdom, and serfdom to employment'. See: Robertson, James (1985: 2006 update) *Future Work: Jobs, Self-Employment and Leisure After the Industrial Age*, Temple Smith/ Gower, London (also see Robertson's 2012 release, *Future Money*)

4   Bannatyne, D (2008) *Wake Up And Change Your Life*, Orion, London

PART 2
CREATING YOUR FREE RANGE LIFE
HOW TO DECIDE WHAT YOU REALLY WANT

3 WHY DOING WHAT YOU LOVE IS NOT NEGOTIABLE

'The more I want to get something done, the less I call it work.' *Richard Bach*

Doing what you love. This is the starting point of any free range life, yet it's a dream that we have been told is a bit of a luxury. Open up almost any business book and the question 'what do you really want to do with your life' doesn't seem to get air time. You could easily get the impression that doing what you love is separate to being successful or earning good money.

Which would be fine, except it doesn't reflect reality.

Study the paths of entrepreneurs and change-makers around the world and a pattern emerges: the ones who do well love what they do. Freaking *adore* it. For example, the late Steve Jobs said, 'You've got to find what you love... The only way to be truly satisfied is to do what you believe is great work. And the only way to do great work is to love what you do.'

Or in the words of Paul Graham, 'it's hard to do a really good job on anything you don't think about in the shower'.[1]

Even people who say publicly that the aim of the game is to make money to fund a certain type of life follow this pattern. Tim Ferriss, in the (otherwise excellent) *The 4-Hour Workweek*[2], suggests that the point isn't loving the work you do, the aim is to find a 'muse' (low time-commitment business) that lets you work as few hours as possible for maximum return on your time. I'm totally behind that last part! But the assumption that you don't need to love what you do to get there is questionable.

Ferris's own 'muse' was a sports supplements venture, and as he explains in his second book, improving how the body works is his biggest interest. He first got known for his approach to finding the most efficient way to get results: something he is passionate about doing every single day in his own life. His, and other people's, successes were not ideas plucked from the air with no relation to their personality or interests.

Doing what you love is not only, you know, *kind of the point of doing this*, but it is your route to making it a success. If you don't love doing something then unless you have superhuman willpower, I guarantee you will end up dropping it no matter how smart a concept it is. I've seen hundreds of perfectly good ideas dropped when someone chose them because they were 'clever' not because they were really, genuinely into them.

Save yourself time and get honest about what you want upfront. The next exercise gets you thinking along these lines. Take time now to scribble your answers to the nine questions.

EXERCISE   **The nine questions**

Brain dump your answers to these questions. No second-guessing or self-editing, just get a pen and write:

1 When you were about 8 years old, the three things you could generally be found doing for play were:

_____

2 The last time you felt alive and completely engaged in the moment was when? Where?:

_____

3 Imagine a genie appeared and offered you 12 months off – with full pay and the security of knowing your job will be waiting for you when you get back. You have a whole year just to do stuff that excites you. What would you do?
Write your answer from the first month, to the last (use another notebook if you run out of space here)

_____

▶

4 Make a note: what is it about each part of your 12 months off that is really exciting to you? For example, if you wrote that you would create art, are you excited about actually making art, or about the place you imagined doing it, or about the people you imagined doing it with?

_____

Don't worry if you're unsure of your answers. These questions are intended to just get your brain into gear for free ranging. In a few chapters' time you can come back to this with a lot more clarity.

The next five questions are a safe space to capture those 'one day' thoughts that might be going through your head. Consider what you think would be awesome to do if only you had all the permission/experience you need and knew it would not fail.

5 Three things I would love to do as a free range career are:

   i _____

   ii _____

   iii _____

6 What excites me about each idea is:

_____

7 What holds me back from each idea is:

_____

8 When I try to make a change I generally:

_____

9 If I had the guts I would (_Really. What would you do?_):

_____

Remember you are not bound to anything you write, so don't hold back.

Now, take a look at what usually goes on when you try to make a change (question 8). Are your usual responses to changing your work throwing up more barriers than solutions? To help you do things differently, here's how to get around a common barrier on the road to discovering what to do with your life: the Idea Death Cycle.

My client Sam spent months in this cycle: she would come up with an idea and then, within seconds, the voice of that inner critic would wipe it out with a cry of 'unfeasible'! Then she would start again: find an idea she liked, think of a reason why not to do it, and go round and round in circles.

That's the way to end up stuck in that office forever. As you'll learn in this book, most ideas don't start out great, they grow that way when given room to breathe. *No one goes from 'I don't know what I want to do' to 'here is the answer together with a bulletproof business plan' in one fell swoop!*

To give yourself the best chance of coming up with a great idea that a) you'll love and b) will work, use this simple technique:

The two-step strategy

The mistake Sam was making was trying to land on an idea that was both *attractive and feasible* all in one go. If it wasn't both, she would give up. However, trying to nail down the practical details the very moment you come up with creative ideas is the fastest way to kill off your very best ideas.

As Professor Richard Wiseman explains in summing up the latest research into creativity, your methodical and critical mind (the conscious brain) is like the loud man in the room. The creative (unconscious) part of your brain is the quiet man – the one that is super-smart and comes up with the juiciest ideas. Problem is, the quiet man backs down the second the loud man starts shouting out reasons why not.[3]

If you want to discover what you really want, you have to give the quiet, innovative mind some space. Here's how to do it.

Use the two-step strategy to separate your dreams from what, at this stage, you think is possible. Step 1: nail down what you want. Step 2: figure out what works, and make it possible.

To help you do this I've separated this book into several sections. This part is exclusively Step 1 thinking. *This is your safe space to dream, and dream big. No idea is too wild in this space.* Don't worry, we will get to the practicalities and checks later (I'm not here to let you go off with a bad idea!) but right now you have full permission to let down the guard and get dreaming.

By starting with the focus on *you* – bringing you alive, getting your brain buzzing with free range potential and filling you with possibilities – we are opening up avenues that linear thinking would never even reach.

Get ready for the ride

The following pages are packed with concepts and techniques that have had the most success in the real world. While some pages might feel a bit 'touchy feely', believe me, I have no patience with pointless fluff. If something is included in this book it is here for a simple reason: it works. *But only if you let it.*

So here's the deal: for the next few chapters, trust in the process, okay? At the end, any objections you have will be waiting and you are free to reclaim them, but for now, all I ask is that you dive in and give it your all. In return, I'll show you a whole new way of seeing your options. Deal?

Brilliant. Let's get started.

4 DREAM BIG – THEN GET OFF YOUR BUTT AND DO IT

'You can't wait for inspiration. You have to go after it with a club.' *Jack London*

Dan was an intelligent man who showed up to one of my courses. I asked him: 'What would you do if you could do anything, anything at all?' He replied: 'Well, I guess I'd work a little bit less, have a bit more time, and not have to do as many spreadsheets.'

A *little* less? A *little* more time? Not do *as much* of something that makes your heart sink? When this is the best dream someone can come up with... you know something has gone seriously wrong. You know that saying, 'aim for the sky and you'll reach the ceiling; aim for the ceiling and you'll stay on the floor'?[4] That's exactly what is happening here.

Want a dream life? It's time to remember how to dream BIG, which is the exact opposite of how the world of work has taught you to behave. So I'd like to show you an example of what can happen when you dare to dream, free range style.

How to quit your job, write a book and get on TV (while baking cakes)

A few years ago, Melissa Morgan was earning a nice salary in a nice job in education in London but she was dreaming of something different. She wanted to:

1 Make and sell beautiful, delicious vegan cupcakes.

2 Open a successful cupcake shop (with no debt) and spread delicious vegan cakes around the country.

3 Then, in an ideal world, she would love to write a cookbook
and have a TV cooking show.

Nice dream, right?

There are so many reasons why these dreams were crazy. For one
thing, Melissa wasn't a trained patisserie chef. For another, she
didn't have business experience – 'I didn't know any of the certifi-
cates or food standards that I needed to get in order to sell what
I made.' Also, she didn't have any funding or the savings to create
a national brand.

So, naturally, Melissa went for it anyway: she donned her frilly
apron and her oversized cupcake-studded hat, took on the persona
of Ms Cupcake: 'a 1950s housewife who calls everyone gorgeous'.
Without quitting her job, she offered to make cupcakes every
chance she got:

> *In the office, if someone was having a leaving do, I'd volunteer
> the cupcakes. Every birthday or dinner I went to I'd bring the
> cupcakes as Ms Cupcake.*
>
> *Even while in a job on weekends I went to nightclubs
> dressed as Ms Cupcake and gave out cupcakes. My aim was
> to make the best vegan cupcakes around, so that even
> a non-vegan would choose them over anything else. While
> I was in my job I worked on them. I got feedback, I kept
> experimenting and improving the recipe until it was just right.*

When she did quit her job she overcame all the lack of business
experience by 'reading up on everything I needed to know about
business and learning on the way'. Within a few months she had her
first market stall, a great brand, and hundreds of loyal customers.
Including me.

The first time I saw Ms Cupcake, who at the time was selling at
my local market, I knew she was going to be big. Her cupcakes
are out of this world – huge, generous, wonderful creations. She had
the most creative recipes – any flavour you want, she'll work out
how to create it. The feeling around her stall was over-the-top and
fabulous. With real personality.

Little did I know that this woomph of personality had come courtesy of Ms Cupcake's Big Dream. She never let herself 'think average' – her dreams allowed her to get clear on what she wanted to share with the world: an experience as much as a cupcake.

Within a year, Ms Cupcake had amassed thousands of loyal fans (including a thriving Facebook page), and the revenue from her cupcakes meant she could open a shop space in Brixton. Everything was self-funded from the sale of cupcakes on her stall that year. At no point did she take a penny of someone else's funding, and she was profitable from the start.

For most people, that alone would be enough of an achievement! However, get this: the rest of her dream is happening too. 'Three publishers made me an offer this year and I just had to choose between them,' she said. Oh, and her TV agent, who is the agent of some of the top TV chefs in the UK, says she is an easy client to place because everyone is asking about her. As we spoke, there was a documentary crew filming in her shop.[5]

Ms Cupcake's advice to you

I don't have a rich partner or a trust fund, I had bills to pay like anyone else. I knew that no one was going to hand me a thriving vegan cupcake business or offer me a deal to write a cookbook just because I said I wanted to.

It was all about believing in my dream and taking action to make sure I got there. So many people say they want those things but you just have to get up and prove yourself.

The fabulous thing about being free range is that you can do this. You don't have to sell yourself to an employer and explain why you're making a career change. You don't need to tick any HR boxes. *You do need the guts to Dream Big and take that first step.*

Dare to dream

Dreamer has become such a negative word. But what if it wasn't? Another word for dreamer is visionary. You'd be hard pressed to find a visionary change-maker who tells you to stop thinking big.

Trying to figure out what you really want without daring to dream is like trying to create the trip of a lifetime but refusing to imagine any destination more than a mile from your home. There is simply no point pretending to aim for a 'dream' life if you haven't let yourself dream in the first place.

The way a free ranger operates is the exact opposite of squishing down your dreams. It is to dream big. SO BIG. And then, to break down that dream and figure out how to make the core happen for real.

EXERCISE   Head in the clouds

First, grab a piece of paper and a pencil, and set a timer for 12 minutes. Now consider this:

Imagine you have been handed a dream free range life. In this fantasy there are no constraints in terms of money, responsibilities, skills or experience. You can do anything at all. The only rule is that everything you include has to fill you with a buzz and make you think 'yes!' (Maybe it will even have you laughing out loud!)

In this fabulous free range life, what would your ideal day look like?

_____

_____

Where would you be?

_____

_____

What would you be doing?

_____

_____

▶

◀

Who would you have around you?

_____

_____

What would happen from morning until evening?

_____

_____

Draw out a typical Head In the Clouds day starting... Now.

_____

_____

Done? The next step is to break down this dream to understand what is really going on behind your answers.

What five themes call to you most strongly in the picture? (For example, when I did this many years back, my picture had a lot of nature/outdoors, a lot of variety, and a big drawing of me speaking in front of groups.)

_____

_____

What is *really* exciting to you about your dream? (For example, if you drew out a picture of you touring the world as a rock star, are you most excited by the thought of being in front of an audience, the music creation or maybe the lifestyle you imagine goes with it?) Write out each 'exciting element' as a separate point:

_____

_____

From now, get in the habit of asking 'why am I really attracted to this idea?' and make a note of the themes you notice. This will build up a strong set of clues that we will use to build your personalized free range solution.

Remember, your dream doesn't have to show a career title yet. Often we get so wound up trying to hit on one all-encompassing 'thing to *do* with the rest of my life', that we forget the importance of lifestyle that comes with it. Yet that's where some of the biggest clues lie.

RESOURCES

Stuck on 'finding your passions'? Read this article for an out-of-the-box perspective on why the search for 'passions' might be getting in the way of you discovering what you love **http://frh.me/f-passions**

MINI CASE STUDY

A key turning point for me was the visualization exercises where I got to imagine my dream life. A year on and I still can vividly recall my answers. Now I've changed from a permanent role at my current job to being a contractor (where I have fewer responsibilities but make more money!), am training as a psychotherapist and building upon my business ideas. I feel so excited about the possibilities before me.

Suzie Chick, London, UK

5 DEFROSTING – YOUR SECRET WEAPON IN FIGURING OUT WHAT YOU WANT

'The intuitive mind is a sacred gift and the rational mind is a faithful servant. We have created a society that honours the servant and has forgotten the gift.'

Albert Einstein

Clara came up to me after a workshop. The moment I saw her I felt the stress. She was rigid and tense, and throughout the workshop she had been feverishly taking notes. She pushed her glasses back up her nose, and said, 'I liked everything you said but I didn't get an answer from the exercises. Is there some sort of test I can do that will tell me what I should do with my life?'

I asked Clara how she had got on with the 'Head in the Clouds' exercise. She opened her notebook (with the name of a major law firm emblazoned on the front), flicked through her notes before looking up, tears welling: 'I couldn't think of anything I wanted to do except sit on the beach and do nothing!'

'That's okay,' I said. 'How about the question on the last time you felt really alive?'

Clara shook her head sadly and said, 'I don't remember. Isn't that stupid? I remember everything else in my life: dates of meetings, names of clients, but I can't remember the last time I felt alive. Is there something wrong with me?'

There was nothing wrong with Clara. Only, it wasn't Clara completing those exercises. The real Clara was frozen, deep down inside the efficient lawyer-Clara. She bubbled up in the moments where Clara would unexpectedly burst into tears but disappeared again when lawyer-Clara berated her for being so silly. *Lawyer-Clara could be a bit of a bitch.*

Lawyer-Clara was great at her work, she knew how to get a promotion and handle a complex case. But she was absolutely terrible at figuring out what would make real-Clara happy. She toned it down, reminded her to 'be careful not to mess up her CV', tried to 'logic' her way to every decision and, in the process, kept Clara away from the single most useful tool for figuring out what she really wanted: her internal GPS.

Your internal GPS is a term used by author and coach Martha Beck to describe that feeling you get when, say, you're about to go into a relationship with someone who turned out to be Really Very Wrong for you, or that 'no!' feeling you got in the first day at that job that turned out to be a bad environment.[6] You *knew* they were wrong, but you couldn't explain why. They looked good on paper. If you're like me (or Clara) you probably said 'don't be so silly, it's just a feeling, I can't turn down the job/leave them'. So you went ahead with the 'yes' when your body was screaming 'no'. *And we both know how that worked out.*

Is your GPS out of whack?

I was speaking with my friend, the fabulous life coach Selina Barker, about this topic and she pointed out that:

At a very early age young kids are vocal about what they want – very firm in their yesses and nos and I wants. Then as we grow up we are told 'you can't have that' so we learn to say no where we wanted to say yes.

Then to please people, or belong, or fit in, we get in the habit of saying no when we mean yes and yes when we mean no.

So when you're asked 'what do you feel inside? What does your gut say?' people will panic and say 'I just don't know!'[7]

Of course you don't know. You've said 'yes' when you meant 'no' (and vice versa) for so long that your internal navigator is completely confused.

Ignoring those feelings is entirely normal (in the career cage). If you didn't say 'no' when you felt 'yes' you might end up marching across to the idiot in the corner office – the one who puts his crappy dance tracks on full volume every afternoon – and finally throwing his stereo out the window. If you let it all flood in, you would feel exactly how wrong things are.

To survive a career that isn't 'you' you've naturally had to put up barriers. You've had to put up a front. You've squished feelings deep down. Now it's time to meet them again. Welcome to *defrosting*.

This might sound off track but there is no way of figuring out what you really want when you aren't sure what 'yes' actually feels like. Without this you could trip over the perfect solution in the street and still be too unsure to go for it.

The first step to connecting with your GPS is to recalibrate your yesses and nos.

EXERCISE   Recalibration

Answer these questions off the top of your head:

I feel wonderful when I spend time with these people:

_____

The last time I did something and time just flew (and I felt alive) was:

_____

The last time I did something that I wish I could do every day was:

_____

My favourite days are:

_____

How do these answers make you feel? For example, when I hit the right answers, I feel elated, with this joy rising up to the top of my head. Others feel a comfortable warmth in their chest, and their body relaxes. Write down your response in as much detail as you can:

_____

▶

Now, flip it over and answer these questions:

I feel dragged down and not good enough when I spend time with:

_____

The last time I did something and time dragged by
(and I felt 'urgh') was:

_____

The last time I did something at work that I wish I never had to do again was:

_____

My least favourite days are:

_____

This is your 'no' state. How does that feel? Where are you feeling it?

_____

From today, start to notice your 'yes' and 'no' moments and pay attention to where and how they happen.

Now, as you go through this book and come across ideas, tap back into that internal GPS. How are you responding? What signals are you getting? Remember there is no point wasting time on an option if you get a big screaming 'no!' inside. That one never works out. By learning to listen to how you're feeling you can shortcut the process of figuring out what you really want, and tap into that really-right path much faster.

6 HOW TO CREATE YOUR PERFECT 'CAREER' WHEN YOU WANT TO DO EVERYTHING

'Ideas are like rabbits. You get a couple and learn to handle them, and pretty soon you have a dozen.'

John Steinbeck

In the previous chapter we explored some ways of tapping in to your dreams. But what do you do when you have lots of little dreams yet no *single* thing that grabs you enough to choose it above the others?

When I was starting out I had trouble deciding what I wanted. There were so many ideas for things I'd love to do, lives I'd want to live, but I couldn't choose. No one idea was perfect and I didn't want to make the wrong decision (again) or close the door on another option.

Since then I've heard the same problem from many clients:

If I launch this consulting business in my home town then I'll miss out on my dream of living in Bali teaching meditation. Also I've always wanted to make documentaries. And breed cats. Maybe. I have no idea how to choose!

Every time you come close to choosing, you worry that you'll get bored after a month. So you give up... Until the next time that your job becomes unbearable. Then the cycle starts again: you fantasize about another life, read a book for inspiration, dare to dream for just a minute... then get stuck. You can't see how to answer the question: 'How can I get someone to pay me to do everything I love?'

Familiar?

Welcome to the 'one thing' myth.

The 'one thing' myth

'I need to choose one thing to do for the rest of my life and I can't start until I find that one perfect job title.'

Myth buster

I just want to get one thing clear here: I think the whole concept of choosing 'one path' off the shelf, and sticking to it for the rest of your life is just nuts. *Totally bonkers.*

You wouldn't assume that you could choose one outfit to wear every day, for every occasion, for the rest of your life and be happy with it. So why assume you can do the same with a career? This is why a lot of people get stuck at the 'deciding' stage. You're looking at all these 'options' out there and putting a lot of pressure on *one* of them being perfect.

Free Range Humans do things differently. They don't expect to find that perfect 'forever outfit'. Instead, they create their own bespoke career, from scratch, by thinking outside the job box. You see:

You *don't* have to get paid directly for something to make it a core part of your business.

If you are a consultant you will not spend each hour of every day consulting. If you teach people organic gardening you are not going to run organic gardening classes all day.

For example:

★ *I don't make my living by being paid to hang out in cafés.* Sitting in cake dens with my laptop, watching the comings and goings, breathing in the aroma, and chatting to lovely people is one of my favourite things, and a core part of my working day. Yet I'm *not* running a café.

★ *I don't make my living by getting paid to teach psychology, social anthropology and linguistics.* Almost everything I do is focused on these very elements: they form a big part of the Free Range Humans approach. Yet no one has *paid* me to be a linguist, or a social anthropologist.

★ *I don't make my living by being paid to write.* Yes I'm writing a book but that isn't a full-time income (and it's also the first time I've agreed to get paid directly to write!). However, I've been writing, almost every day, as part of my business for years.

From guest articles and blog posts (which bring in traffic), to courses I've written, to stories that illustrate my Free Range Friday emails, several times a week I manage to write and tell stories in a way I love and, as you will learn in Part 4, this fun project has grown my business massively.

★ *I don't get paid to travel the world.* In the last year alone I have travelled to the United Kingdom, United States, Bali, Laos, Cambodia, Malaysia, Italy, Thailand, Hong Kong and Australia and run my business from there. This book was written in five different countries! Yet no one is paying me to travel.

★ *I don't get paid to meet incredible people, be enthusiastic or do creative photo and video projects.* But I integrate these into my day and they enhance what I do get paid for (a portfolio career that includes freeing career-cage-trapped humans!)

There's a myth out there that the only way to do what you love as a career is to get paid directly for that activity. Kind of like in a job (which is most people's only model of making an income). So, if you like travel and writing, the career-cage answer is to be a travel writer (like thousands of others out there). If you can't get that, then you have to give up.

But working for yourself is not like having a job – when you are free range, the thing you get paid for directly is often not what takes up the bulk of your time. Ask anyone who does well as a solo-preneur, and they will say that *growing their business* is a core part of how they spend their days. Some people (conventional business types) find this part boring. Free Range Humans see it as an excuse for getting playful.

To grow your business, you might end up writing, filming, giving talks, baking cakes (I know someone who did this as a promotional idea!), meeting lots of fascinating people (the ones currently on your 'dream dinner' list), or an endless range of other options. With no boss to set the agenda, you get to choose what you do.

Knowing this, here are three out-of-the-box approaches you can use to create your perfect free range solution:

1 Create a bespoke career.

2 Create a portfolio career.

3 Create an evolving career.

1. Create a bespoke career

Have you ever walked into a clothes shop, seen a mannequin with an outfit that looks amazing, and tried on the whole thing from top to toe? I have. It didn't look right at all. It's one thing to get inspiration from the shop floor, but then you need to add that scarf, remove those boots, find a different top... and then it looks just perfect.

The truth is that you are unique. Perfect-fit careers are not 'found', they are created from scratch, tweaked and tailor-made to suit you in all your uniqueness.

When I first became a coach I realized I didn't exactly love everything about coaching. For example, I'm not one to sit back, listen and nod while someone car crashes their life, or restrain enthusiasm when it's clear you've hit on something fabulous. For months I was so stressed about this: every session I felt like I had to pretend to be someone else (someone more passive) in order to fit the box of the conventional coaching world. I felt as if I wasn't good enough because I was different.

So, after spending far too long packing my personality into a box, I decided to turn my natural style into an advantage – not hide it, out of fear it might be a liability.

I came out as myself: as your feisty Free Range Humans guide. Now, it's less 'and what do *you* think?' and more strategies, ideas, brainstorming inspiration and a dose of straight talking (with love). I joke, I laugh, I ask the big questions, I say it like it is. Occasionally I swear. *Try finding that in a job description.*

Result? Way happier. To my surprise, this honesty and new ways of connecting with people landed me with a bunch more clients too. This is a common occurrence when free rangers break the rules and come out as themselves rather than following the beige crowd.

Other changes I made (which others said were impossible) include location-freeing a conventionally one-location business, and integrating creativity to promote my business: such as drawing the little chicken logo that still hangs out on the Free Range Humans blog. That increases my business and, at the same time, is so much fun I'd do it for free.

Getting the picture? What other people do is not your job description. You can and should tailor ideas to suit you.

EXERCISE **Tailoring To Fit**

Steps to tailor free range careers to fit:

1 List out your favourite ideas for a free range career. These ideas don't need to be perfect, just list out the ones you found in some way attractive:

_____

_____

2 Identify the elements of each idea that have held you back from choosing that one for sure (ie What about it do you think will not be so fun? What parts of it are you concerned might not suit your personality?).

_____

_____

3 Taking inspiration from my example, above, how could you change each idea so that your personality and preferences are a benefit rather than a liability?

_____

_____

▶

4 Look at your ideas list now. Is there any way you can integrate several of your ideas into one solution? For example, if you are attracted to both x and x, you could potentially combine those to x. Brainstorm possible combinations below.

_____

_____

5 Looking back over what you have come up with in steps 3 and 4, is there any option that now seems particularly attractive? Circle the ones you could potentially see yourself moving forward with and getting excited about!

_____

_____

If nothing fits perfectly now, don't worry. Come back to this exercise as you progress throughout this book and get more inspiration. Continue to add to your list and 'tailor' using these techniques until you create a solution that truly ticks your boxes.

MINI CASE STUDY

I had been a dreamer all my life, but never found a job to match my dreams. For example, I wanted to write about sex but had never found a job that asked for this – especially in the academic circles I have been working in for the last 10 years. I finally realized that I didn't have to wait for a job to show up – I could create my own role as a sex writer. I've set up a business supporting women to enjoy their sexuality, have two websites, and I have a publisher interested in my first novel. My advice: start small but dream big!

Anna Samson, Devon, UK
www.ladygardenproject.com

2. Create a portfolio career

Can't fit all of your ideas into one solution? You'll love this.

There is a growing tribe of humans out there who get paid to do more than one thing. There's even a name for this: portfolio careers. A portfolio career is where you do more than one type of thing, and get paid for it. You might be a writer, an image consultant and teach yoga. As Barrie Hopson and Katie Ledger point out in their book *And What Do You Do? 10 Steps To Creating A Portfolio Career* (2009), a portfolio career is not the same thing as having a few ideas and not being able to make a success of any one of them, it is a conscious choice that lets you achieve a work blend that fits:

> *When Elisavet Sotiriadou quit her job as a BBC broadcast producer and journalist, she combined her love of music journalism, Greek food and DJing to create a bespoke portfolio career. Her London-based Greek cookery classes started out when she gathered together friends from Facebook and via email, and have grown organically to the point where they sell out and she has been written up in national magazines and newspapers – and she has cooked on national TV.*
>
> *Now she has expanded her portfolio, including Greek supper clubs as well as doing catering and being hired as a private chef.*
>
> *However, as Elisavet says, had she tried to find the 'one perfect thing' to do, she would never have started the classes as they didn't look like they could make any money. By including cooking as part of her portfolio career, this small side project got room to grow. As a portfolio careerist she still does this alongside her music journalism (interviewing acts such as Lionel Richie, June Tabor and The Killers).*

The wonderful thing about a portfolio career is that, just like Elisavet, you get to constantly edit your career when you get bored – you can add in one strand today that you decide to wind down a year down the line, and you can replace that with something else, without going through a huge career change.

3. Create an evolving career

Becoming a Free Range Human isn't like a career change into another 'job sector'. You don't have to choose one business and stick to that, and *only* that, for 10 years.

The truth is that if you're someone who loves variety and change, odds are you would never be happy doing one thing, and only one thing, forever. So quit pretending that's even an option for you. I was chatting about this with the wonderful Barbara Winter, author of *Making A Living Without A Job.*[8] Barbara has been self-employed for 38 years and has had more strands to her career than most people have ideas.

'Who said you had to do one thing for the rest of your life?' she asked. 'You're choosing for this year's version of you, not the 10 years in the future version of you. Who *knows* what that person will want?'

When you learn how to be a Free Range Human you are learning the tools to launch whatever you like, and edit your business so it continues to grow with you. You're building a flexible vessel for your life, so choosing the right general direction of the vessel is all that matters: you can correct the details along the way.

A single job in which you do just one thing? Squeezing yourself into someone else's job description? Outdated. Now *you* have control. When no one job fits, it's time to create your own bespoke free range career.

MINI CASE STUDY

I used to define myself by my job title and the company I worked for – but now if someone asks me 'what do you do', I *love* the fact that I can say 'I do a few things actually... I'm an HR consultant, photographer, aspiring coach and also a school governor'. It's nice to be openly multi-dimensional. I feel much 'free-er', and since making the move from career-cage to free range, I'm now earning as much if not more than I was before but only working for half the time, meaning I can spend more precious time with my family.

Frank Mason, Solihull, UK

Reflection

What have you realized from this chapter? Capture your thoughts about each option in the table below:

	Why I find this attractive	*How I could use this*
1 *Bespoke career*		
2 *Portfolio career*	eg: because I have two ideas I am keen to do and couldn't decide between them!	eg: start out with consulting in my current field while building up my idea for public speaking workshops
3 *Evolving career*		

FREE RANGE ACTION   Get a taste of free range life

Connie Hozvicka, a Free Range Human you will meet later in this book, says:

When I decided I was going to go free range, the most powerful thing I did was creating a mini-version of the life I wanted while still in my job. I wasn't ready to quit there and then, but while I was getting ready, I could change who I spent time with. So I made a point of avoiding the negative people in the office. When I had to see them, I would politely refuse to get drawn in to their negative conversations.

I did other things, like took a day off and went to a café with my laptop, and did exactly what I imagined I would do on a free range day. In the evenings I made time to create art: that was all part of my dream picture.

These actions got me into the mindset of making up my own rules. You can't come up with ideas and just dream about them, you have to live them.

Many other free rangers have similar stories. For example, in the months before leaving my last job I got permission to get out and work on a project by myself in the downstairs Starbucks. Sure it was a chain in an underground shopping mall but this taste of free range life made a big difference. I asked for permission 'just this once', and then it turned into a regular assumption that I would pop down there once every few days.

These actions help you get aware of what does and does not work for you, and many people find that shaking up their routine allows for unexpected ideas to show up. It also gives you a taste of creating the life you want, like a real Free Range Human.

Now it's your turn. Change something in your life this week to bring it in line with your dream. For example, if 'variety' is one of your themes, do something as small as taking a new route to work. If spending time with certain types of people came up as important, find them (be it through friends or discovering an event where they gather), and get out of your usual circles for an hour this week.

▶

What are three free range actions you could take over the next three weeks?

_____

_____

Which _one_ do you want to make happen this week?

_____

_____

HINT If you think an action is too inaccessible simply ask 'how would a Free Range Human make this happen?' and go and do that.

RESOURCES

For more on choosing what you want and creating a bespoke career, get my free audio on 'How To Create Your Own Career When No One Job Fits' at **http://www.free-range-humans.com/doeverything** To go sraight to this audio, scan the QR code with your smartphone or tablet.

7 SPOT YOUR SUPERPOWERS

'Freedom means finding a home for all your talents.'

Scott Ginsberg

There's one more piece of the puzzle to creating your perfect free range solution: *you*. How can you have above average – scrap that, a *fabulous* – life if you believe you are nothing but average? Answer: you can't. To get an inspiring free range career, you need to start getting comfortable with your secret superpowers. Get this:

1 You are not the sum of your 'learned skills'.

2 You do have something special to offer the world.

3 And you don't have to be the next Mozart for that to be true.

All of which might be a bit different from the way you've been taught to think about yourself so far.

You see, from a young age you've been sold a lie. That lie is that you have to be good at *everything* in order to be 'good enough'. When you were at school and getting that report card, where was the focus: on the subjects you were great at or the ones that 'need work'? If you got private tuition was it for subjects at which you were amazing or the ones that you are not so great at? In the workplace and your annual appraisal where is the focus?

You know the answer. The focus is always on the weaknesses, it's about getting you up to average. The bits where you shine, the parts you find natural, those are put to one side. You are 'good enough' at that already, the logic goes. I call this the 'all-rounder' myth.

As a Free Range Human you're going to have to flip that right around. By focusing on your strengths, you tap into your shortcut to loving what you do and standing out in the process.

Average is no longer an option

Mediocrity is what happens when you squash down your greatest strengths in the name of trying to be someone you're not. Ditto with unhappiness, dissatisfaction and the absence of joy. Those feelings all come from disregarding your strengths (because they feel too easy).

Easy does not mean lazy. Ease simply means you're doing something completely in flow with who you are. The moment you think that something feels too easy and too fun to be of value to others, take note. That's often the moment people hit upon their greatest thing.

Imagine, just for a moment, if you took all the time you spent struggling against the things you find difficult, tedious and soul-sapping and put *that same time and energy* into doing something that comes naturally to you, something that you do as second nature and that makes you feel wide-awake alive. Imagine how much of an advantage you'd have then. That's why strengths are so important in making a change: tap into your strengths and you can get up to speed in months, rather than battling for years.

> 'But I already know my strengths and I don't want to use them anymore.'

If you don't like using them, they are not strengths. When we talk about strengths we are not talking about them in the sense of the way the word is used in the workplace, where strengths are often used to mean 'something you are pretty good at'.

There is a difference between strengths and skills. Skills are something you have learnt (and got good at). You don't necessarily love them. Strengths are innate: you have always done them in one form or another (these are your natural points of excellence).

For example, Jill and Dave are both good at corporate presentations. They have both learnt the skills involved and can do it well. However do they *both* have a strength of speaking in public?

Since a young age Jill has always grabbed the microphone and loved being in front of the audience. In contrast, Dave doesn't particularly love being in front of an audience. However, he has put in a lot of time and effort to the point where he is fine with it and gets nice feedback. Here's the difference: when Jill gets off the stage her energy is sky high, she can't imagine being anywhere else and is on a high for days! When Dave gets off the stage he feels drained. He is proud that he did a good job... but he is happy it's over. Jill's best results come when people see her on stage. Dave's best results come from his detailed analysis at his desk. Jill and Dave both have the skill of giving corporate presentations but Jill has the strength of being a natural speaker.

You can tell the difference between your own skills and strengths in this way. If it's just a skill it will always feel like a bit of a struggle, even when you get good at it. Also, you won't think 'I can't believe people *pay* me to do something this fun!'

This is what makes your true strengths so hard to spot: it feels too easy so you might well overlook it. For example, my client Alex was a natural people person: it was blindingly obvious to me that his 'best thing' was bringing together a team. He did it without thinking, and both in and out of work he loved nothing more than making sure everyone was getting on. However, Alex worked in a highly technical field so he put all his energy into getting good at his technical skills: he didn't believe there was any point talking about his people-based strengths. One day I asked him 'how do you feel about the people who get paid to manage groups?' He replied, 'I look down on those sorts of roles, to be honest. What they do is fun, it's not real work.' I then put him in touch with another client who had opposite strengths and who, despite years of 'skills training' in people management, still found the people-side of the job to be a struggle. That was when Alex realized that what was 'easy and fun' for him was a valuable asset to others.

Alex is not alone. When I work with clients I can almost guarantee that the very thing they say is 'not that valuable' is the biggest thing they have to offer. This happens because the dominant view of work in our culture is shaped by the Anglo-Saxon Protestant work ethic, which tells us that for something to be worthwhile it has to be hard.[9] This means we habitually disregard our own very best thing for being 'too easy', or we assume that 'everyone can do that'. The truth is that you are not like other people. For each thing you would poke your eye out to avoid, other people are right now reading a copy of this book to try to figure out how to get *paid* to do just that.

The final indicator of a strength is that you are doing it already (even if you don't notice). Although Alex assumed he had risen through the ranks because of his technical skills, he soon realized all his most satisfying successes came back to the way he pulled a team together and made lasting connections. Once you discover your hidden superpowers, a lot of your backstory will make much more sense (and your future path clears up as well).

So how can you find your strengths? Simple: identify your weaknesses.

Weaknesses are just strengths in the wrong environment

This is such an important point: it is quite possible that the very parts of your personality that you try to hide away at work are the parts that hold the key to your hidden superpowers.

For example, before I changed career back in the job world I thought I had a huge weakness of constantly wanting to change how things were done. I came up with new ideas all the time for how we could improve the status quo. My boss wasn't interested: he wanted me to focus on the job at hand, which had nothing to do with creating change. My constant need to make things bigger and better – and never settling for average – was a weakness when I was supposed to just keep things ticking over quietly.

Then, I changed career into consultancy. Suddenly my job was to see how things could be done differently, push the status quo, to come up with big ideas. That old weakness, which I had spent years trying to keep down, became a strength that businesses were paying a lot of money for! Plus, I got better results from the first month than I had got in years of painstakingly trying to 'get good enough' at something that was against my nature. This was *fun*.

You have several masked strengths in your life, too. Let's say you have been kicking yourself for having the weakness of not being able to focus on just one thing: you bounce between projects too fast, and feel like you can't focus. However, your job tells you to settle down, do one thing at a time, so you are always berating yourself for being too scatty!

Now imagine an environment where that *exact trait* is a benefit.

I'll tell you a place where this would be an advantage: a brainstorming session. Being able to move between options fast – and not get bogged down in details – is a huge advantage in brainstorming. Turns out that weakness ('being unfocused') was masking the strengths of being able to be a fast-moving, adaptable, big-picture thinker with lots of ideas.

Voila. We have just turned your weakness into a strength.

EXERCISE   **Flip It**

To find your hidden strengths follow these four steps to fill out the table on the next page:

1 Write out five things that you currently think of as weaknesses. Include things you can't help doing, tell yourself you should stop doing, or wish you could change and do better.

2 Next, ask yourself: 'What is really behind this weakness?' *As in the example above, if your weakness is 'I can't focus on one project at a time', the driver behind that might be 'I love constant stimulation and my mind moves fast'. Getting to the personality trait behind the 'weakness' lets you think about it in a more balanced way.*

3 Now scribble down two situations where each of these traits would be an advantage. *In the example above, this was the brainstorming session. Remember these situations don't have to be 'viable career options', the point is to know they exist. This step gets your mind moving to discover possibilities where you can add value by being you.*

4 Finally, write down the hidden strength/s you have just unmasked. *For the example above, the strengths listed might include 'big-picture thinker' and 'adaptable' (among others).*

▶

◀

1. 'Weaknesses' (things I tell myself I should improve/stop doing)	2. Underlying personality trait (what is really behind this 'weakness'?)	3. Advantage environments (two situations where this trait would be an advantage)	4. Hidden strength (the strength/s this weakness was masking)

How to use your strengths to find your thing

When you identify your strengths, here are two ways you can use them to create a great free range career:

1. Make it yours

If five different people launched a pet-care company they would all do it in different ways: one person would round-up a team and make connections with lots of people; another would write intelligently about it and sell the information online; another would form close relationships with individual pet owners; another may provide a daycare service to high-end pooches, in an environment where every detail was taken care of; another might create dog meet-ups around the world, with a festival environment and puppy-tinis for all.

Your strengths don't necessarily tell you what to do. They enable you to do whatever you want to do better than anyone else, because you'll do it your way. On your own terms. Can you add in your strengths to enhance your idea to suit you more and stand out from the norm? If there is something in your idea that you know just isn't 'you' can you take it out and replace it with a strength?

2. Create value by being yourself

Whatever you find easy and fun, someone else thinks of as a chore. That means that you could build a business around a few strengths with which others struggle. However, it is more than likely that you are overlooking those strengths simply because they are so easy for you.

For example, when Rachel Papworth came to me, she had, in her words, 'become embarrassed' about her love of decluttering and organizing. However, as she worked through the free range exercises, she realized that her 'skills and passion are valuable to many people' and so she launched herself as a professional declutterer. 'Now I get paid for something I used to hide away! Creating 'Green and Tidy' has led me to not just embracing this side of my personality but shouting about it from the rooftops.'[10]

As Einstein said: 'Everyone is a genius. But if you judge a fish on its ability to climb a tree it will spend its whole life believing it is stupid.' Chances are, to date you've been focusing on climbing that tree with your fins and wondering why it's not feeling right. Now's your chance to change all that.

BONUS   **Personality profiles**

Struggling to find your strengths? Figuring it out yourself is an interesting exercise but the most useful results come from a good personality profile assessment. I get all my clients to discover their personality profiles no matter what stage they are at: it's almost impossible to create a great free range career without this awareness.

▶

From figuring out what to do, to getting started, to taking off and shining, you have simply got to know who you are (and who you are not). Your personality profile is a shortcut to discovering what you really have to offer the world and where you'll be happier in the process. A good assessment can also save you months or years of struggle by showing you which strategies work best for your personality.

To find your personality profile, check out this page for my recommendations. Not all assessments are created equal so I have handpicked the profile systems I like to use for myself and my clients:
http://frh.me/personalityassessments
To go straight to this personality profile assessment, scan the QR code with your smartphone or tablet.

BONUS   **Free range personality**

Is there a certain type of person better suited to free ranging? Anyone can do it but there are a few consistent tendencies that crop up in Free Range Humans. See how you score!
http://frh.me/freerangepersonality
To go straight to the Free Range personality profile, scan the QR code with your smartphone or tablet.

TIP   **Idea generation strategies**

If you're buzzing with an idea or two already, skip this part! But if you want more, here are five ways to come up with great free range ideas:

1. Solve your own problem

Start noticing opportunities to scratch your own itch. This is how Corie Hardee, founder of Little Borrowed Dress, came up with her idea:

The idea behind Little Borrowed Dress came where I do most of my best thinking: in front of my closet. Rather than deciding what to wear, I had the less glamorous task of choosing what not to wear, specifically what to toss. The main offenders: bridesmaid dresses.

The four bridesmaid dresses were the most expensive items in my closet, yet each had been worn exactly once. That's when I thought, this is nuts, men can rent tuxedos, why can't women RENT bridesmaid dresses? I started Little Borrowed Dress to make that a possibility.[11]

Try this for yourself. Identify one to three topics that you have learnt about or experienced in the last few years. Be it a personal life experience (such as getting out of debt) or something else. *What help would you have wanted with those topics at the time?* Now, crucially: are you personally excited about offering this sort of help to people who were in your position? If so, scratch your own itch and create that solution.

2. Zoom in and take off

As Twitter co-founder Evan Williams says, 'the specialist will almost always kick the generalist's ass'. Spot something offered to a wide market and think of ways you can tailor it perfectly for a small section of that market and in the process snaffle up 100 per cent of that group's interest.

3. Check your back pocket

When I coach clients on finding their idea, we can spend a whole session talking through options but I can almost guarantee that what they will end up doing is that little throwaway idea they mention in the last five minutes of the session. It's uncanny. The person will say that they have a 'little idea' but that it is too obvious, or maybe too crowded. Then I ask them to tell me about it, and they light up with excitement. That's when I know we're on to the winner.

Over the next few chapters you might discover some techniques that could make the impossible possible, so check your back pocket and write down anything you've been holding back.

4. Think like a free ranger

You've reached this far in the book so in my eyes you are officially a free range fledgling. Congratulations. Just by taking on these new ideas you are already thinking differently from 90 per cent of people who stare mournfully out the office window. So, you are no longer limited to thinking up job titles: now, you can turn an idea, an interest, or even a lifelong trait – such as 'I like making people feel beautiful' – into a career.

To make this happen, *start to think of how you'd like to add value to the world*. Most people just think of a 'topic' (such as 'counselling' or 'dog training') but free rangers add in the *lifestyle* they want and *what they bring to the picture* personally.

5. Get out of your comfort zone

If you are constantly moving in the same social circles, chances are you're not encountering many new ideas. Make a point of going to ideas and creative events in your area – or even joining online courses – and meeting people who do things differently from the people you spend time with right now. What two things can you do this week that take you out of your usual habits and get you exposed to new people?

MINI CASE STUDY **From legal marketer to adult educator**

I spent years searching for that 'perfect' alternative career, hoping for inspiration but frankly getting nowhere. Then I realized that I just had to get out of my comfort zone before anything would change. So I did a short course on teaching English as a second language (ESOL). That led to meeting new people, a new environment and, at last, some new ideas. I am now creating my own course, which I will deliver to adult learners next month, something I would never have thought of before. I am moving in a completely new direction – it's scary, it's challenging but it feels great!

Michael Devine, London, UK

FREE RANGE PROFILE
BENNY'S STORY – 'TRAVEL THE WORLD, LEARN LANGUAGES, AND MAKE A LIVING FROM YOUR BLOG'

At the time, I was working as a translator, which was good but time consuming. I had to work long hours to come close to making enough money.

One day I was in Thailand and ran into a bunch of full-time bloggers and location independent people. They saw I was stressed out because I had to work eight hours a day on a party island while they were lying on the beach. I had my own blog then, but it was just a personal side project. It was just me, tracking my journey learning languages in three months. But over the last few months it had grown a lot of traffic and when I started talking to these bloggers, it turned out my blog was bigger than some of theirs!

They suggested I stop working so much and make money from my blog, but I said no, I didn't want to put ads all over it, that would have taken away from the message. Instead they gave me another idea: write an e-guide to how to learn a language quickly, the way I had taught myself. So I did just that.

Within a month I had created the language hacking guide, a multimedia product. It has since been translated into 24 languages. There are worksheets and hours of audio interviews with the Internet's most famous language learners. I thought at first that this $97 e-guide would be a sideline, but since the day of release, every cent I earned in the last two years has been from that one digital product.

I now blog regularly on **www.FluentIn3Months.com.** *At the moment it's about me in Taiwan learning Mandarin in three months. The appeal is that I am not naturally talented with languages – I did quite poorly with languages at school, and I'm upfront about the fact I don't even like the process of learning languages! What I love is to get the learning over fast so I can speak fluently, travel and hang out with the locals.*

That's how a lot of people feel too. You want to be comfortable speaking socially, not be stuck learning grammar for years. I show them that this can be done, from zero to chatting comfortably in three months. In fact you can speak from day one. I help people achieve this by writing about my experiences and showing videos of my progress, even the bad parts.

My mission is to get more people learning languages: it isn't expensive, it's something you can do at home at any age and you don't have to have a talent for it. I learned Italian while working a 63-hour a week job. The appeal of this message, and the draw of watching my progress and my videos, means I get a lot of social media shares, decent traffic, and the guide sells off the back of that. Now the number of hours I put in no longer has a relationship with the number of zeros in my bank account. That gives me a lot of freedom.

Benny Lewis, Ireland
www.FluentIn3Months.com

8 TAKING FREE RANGE ACTION

'Do not wait to strike until the iron is hot.
Make it hot by striking.'

WB Yeats

This chapter is a bit different: you can take a deep breath, there's no soul searching or deep thinking (phew!)

No one figures out their perfect path *just* by thinking about it. To hone in on what you really want, thinking has to be backed up by a big dose of action. That's why I shared Benny's story. Benny is an action taker. When he had the idea for his blog, he had the domain name registered and the outline up within 12 hours, and was getting his first language challenge under way within 24 hours. Miles away from the six months of research that people often assume are essential before taking the first step!

Which raises an important point: what exactly should you do when you have an idea for a free range career?

The 'endless research' myth

'I think I need to research it a bit more first. If I keep reading up on the options I'm bound to stumble on the answer.'

My client Liz was going round in circles. She would have an idea, fire up the search engine and end up spending hours at her computer, night after night, going down a research hole trapped in analysis paralysis. There were so many pros and cons, so many what ifs, the more she researched the more confused she got.

Myth buster

STOP. Do not pass the library door. Do not collect 200 websites. Desk research is addictive. It gives you the illusion of moving forward but in reality keeps you mired in analysis paralysis. There is always something more to learn. Always another 'what if'. And at the end you still don't know what it's like on the ground. That's why no one discovers their path through doing more research.

As a bit of a bookworm I was surprised to discover that in many situations humans make better decisions with *less* information. For example, there's a study that showed doctors make better decisions about treating back pain when they had fewer information points to go on. The ones who were given all the information they wanted, via detailed MRI scans, were misled by 'red herrings' and making bad decisions.[12]

Our conscious brains simply can't handle considering large amounts of information at the same time. Plugging in too much information is like running all the applications on a computer at once: you either get fixated on one minor point, or go into overload, freeze up, and end up more confused than before.

If you can't see the woods for the trees, the answer isn't to add more trees.

Free range third way

What can you do instead of endless research? Welcome to the world of prototype projects. Prototype projects are core to free ranging – you can use them to figure out what you want, to get started and, even after you launch, you run small projects to try out new ideas without fear of failure. The typical free range business is built from a dream, followed by a series of prototype projects taking you from here to there.

For example, Ms Cupcake, who we met in Chapter 4, began with the simple project of baking cupcakes and handing them out at the office. Then she did the same at clubs. Then she started a market stall. Then the next step and the next. *Starting in mini steps made her big dream happen.* That's much smarter (and, counterintuitively, faster) than trying to go from 'no idea' to 'perfect bulletproof business concept' in one sitting!

There are two types of prototype projects: Play Projects[13] and Test Projects. The Play Project helps you figure out if you would really love doing this idea, and the Test Project figures out if it will work in reality (and how to tweak it so that it does work). In a Play Project you look *inside* yourself and in a Test Project you look *outside* yourself. So, Ms Cupcake's first time baking in the office would have been a Play Project (to see how it felt and if it was a good fit). When she did it again – to notice people's interest in different types of cupcakes, and refine the recipes – that was a Test Project.

This chapter is your chance to start on a Play Project.

The aim of a Play Project

The aim of a Play Project is to discover whether or not you enjoy doing your idea in reality.

Importantly, this project's success is not judged by whether or not you continue with it after the first round: sometimes, the end result is that you discover that your idea wasn't quite what you expected and so you save yourself months of thinking 'what if' (a valuable outcome in itself). For example, like Ms Cupcake, I used to have dreams of being a cake-preneur: I liked baking and was always the one showing up with a plate of baked goodies to the party. It seemed a natural idea! So, I created a little website (made by myself overnight, as you will learn, too), contacted people running local events and volunteered to cater.

The first two or three times it was brilliant fun... and then it quickly turned into a chore. I discovered that while I love baking, I don't really like having to create that many cakes so often (for such little return) – my version of fun was the process of *building the brand*, and creating a positive experience, not so much having to fiddle around with frosting for six hours at a time. So, I ended up dropping that idea and building from that discovery to focus on what does work for me. *Diving in and doing the project taught me more than I learnt in 18 months of dreaming and researching.* It also let me let go of the idea of being a cake-preneur, allowing my other ideas on the shortlist to fill that space. Plus, as a result of this project I met some people who ended up having an impact on the business I did go ahead with.

Play Projects can also turn into something more. The original Free Range Humans blog was started as my personal Play Project, and built up into something much bigger than I ever expected. The fact that you're reading this book is evidence of where a project can go!

Play Projects take the pressure off the idea that you have to decide for sure before you start something. You don't know where this will go – but start now, notice what happens and I guarantee you will discover more than you would in a month of 'thinking about it'.

FREE RANGE ACTION   **Your first project**

John Williams, the author of *Screw Work, Let's Play*, is (unsurprisingly) a huge fan of Play Projects. Here is how he suggests you choose your first project:

1. Choose a project that excites you

Identify a free range career idea that you have been toying with. Then choose a way to get started on that in short project form. As John explains:

> the aim is to produce something based on the part of this idea that is most exciting to you, *be it your first portrait photo shoot, your first 3 blog posts, your first YouTube videos. For example, if you think you might want to be a wedding planner, volunteer to get involved in a friend's wedding; your results can be written feedback or your written summary of the event.*

Remember, this is a Play Project not a 'planning project'. As John says, 'if you want to write a blog, *don't* make your project choosing the logo or researching the topic. Get a free layout and get those first posts up.' If you want to teach public speaking, your Play Project is *not* creating business cards or 'talking to people who do it already to see what it's like': it is finding three people to whom you can teach public speaking and *actually* doing it. All those other parts can come later should you decide to continue.

▶

2. Cut it down to a project that can be completed in a clear timeframe

John advises that 'your project must be one you can start and finish in 30 days maximum. Any longer the whole thing gets overwhelming and probably you'll never start if you're uncertain already.'

I'll go a step further and suggest that if you know you tend to put things off, then make your first project something you can start and finish in *one week*.

You can extend your next project if you choose, but by choosing a shorter timeframe you: a) get faster results, and b) can decide more easily (after all, this is only for the week not for life!) Your project is too big for a week, or even for 30 days? Simply cut it down to a part you can do in that timeframe. The aim is not to launch a business it is to get started and get a feel for what it is actually like to do what you are currently just thinking about.

3. Produce something tangible at the end

Identify what you want to have to show at the end. For example, as John suggests, if you were writing that blog, your outcome could be your first three posts published. If you were running the public speaking workshop, then it could be participant feedback, or your notes for the sessions.

4. Schedule it in

Give yourself two days from today to finalize what this project will be and what you will deliver at the end. Then, mark the end date in your diary.

HINT   Everyone who does this has a busy life. Don't wait for that perfect free weekend (it will never come). Instead, schedule in 30 minutes three evenings a week, set it aside as your ringfenced free range time and commit to keeping those appointments with yourself, no matter what.

5. Start

Now. And, as you go, stay curious throughout: what is working for you? What do you keep putting off? Which part is resistance and which part is you screaming: 'No, this is wrong!' Which part feels so right you didn't want to stop doing it? Take notes and build up a picture of your responses.

The aim of this is to get you feeling alive. None of this 'oh I think I might maybe sort of like it' blandness – a real live 'woah I completely love this and I have to keep doing it' feeling. That's an indicator of what you really want to do if I ever saw one.

So: what are you going to do for your first mini project? Tweet your project to @FreeRangeHumans with hashtag #freerangeproject to let us know how you're going!

MINI CASE STUDY

Coming across the idea of prototype projects was a turning point. I started a pop-up cinema project that had been germinating in the back of my mind for a while. I didn't know where it would go when I ran that first film night, but when I look back I see that it changed everything.

Gradually my little 'hey, let's put on a show, right here in the barn!' idea has grown: I'm now doing it with two friends and we've put on a film every month for the last 18 months. Someone gave us a screen and a DVD player, most of the venues we use are given free, and we have built quite a following. We've done it all in our spare time. I can see the possibility of this becoming my career... and even got up the courage to resign from a job that was burning me out.

Melanie Pearson, Sheffield, UK

A word from your inner critic

'*Doing a Play Project? Listening to yourself? You don't have time for that! Stop being so selfish.*'

'*Ha ha, you still don't have a proper dream! It's pathetic: You don't know what you want at your age. Grow up.*'

'*Those are your strengths? Everyone wants to do that! Who are you to think you can get paid for that?*'

Familiar? Meet your inner critic.

Your inner critic is the voice in your head that tells you you're not good enough – it criticizes your appearance, your worthiness,

this book), feel free to come back to this page and add
...vers as your true picture emerges.

...l [accessed 15 March 2011] The Top Idea In Your Mind.
...ulgraham.com/top.html

...ny (2007) *The 4-Hour Workweek: Escape 9-5, live any-*
...*the new rich*, Crown Archetype, New York

...the 'Loud Man' idea in his book *59 Seconds: Think*
...*a lot* (2009). For more research on unconscious and
...ssing, a good starting point is Nobel prize-winner
...'s *Thinking, Fast and Slow* (2011).

...o the football manager Bill Shankly.

...s Cupcake's story here because of her free range
...ing barriers and making dreams a reality. Despite
...hysical shop location, all her other actions fitted
...d. Had she chosen to make this an online shop
...would have made a success of that as well. In all
...y fits: no funding even for the shop, no employees
...year and, indeed, she supported herself full-time
...the shop opened: in sum, don't feel you need
...going! http://www.mscupcake.co.uk

...on internal GPS I highly recommend her book
...*b Star* (2003).

...ker's wise words can be found at
...om

...*Making A Living Without A Job: Winning*
...*you love(Revised)*, Bantam, New York
...*testant Ethic and the Spirit of Capitalism*,

...ygreenandtidylife.co.uk.

...earned From A Four-Time Bridesmaid',
...nforb.es/x8jJMB

...009/02/mri_and_back_pain.php

...used by John Williams in *Screw Work*
...e I was starting to use prototype pro-
...it is far better than mine, so thanks to

...*Verbatim* (revised), February 1992,

your potential. It's the voice that tells you that you can't really have
what you want and no one really likes you (and yes, you are too
fat). It speaks to you in a way you wouldn't speak to a friend.

Author and therapist Frederick Perls describes your inner critic
(which he calls your Top Dog) as usually 'righteous and authoritar-
ian: he knows best'. As Perls explains, 'the Top Dog is a bully...
he manipulates with demands and threats of catastrophe, such as,
"if you don't, then – you won't be loved, you won't get to heaven,
you will die," and so on.'[14]

Why are we talking about this?

Any challenge to the status quo, any attempt to actually get up and
do something you love, is going to get this critical Top Dog growling.
And that's probably going to happen right around... now.

If you pretend that figuring out what you want and making a
change is just a tick-the-box 'rational brain' process, you're setting
yourself up for a fall. *If your inner critic's fatalist words win your
head space, you will give up.* He will be making an appearance on
this journey, so let's deal with that.

We all have a Top Dog/inner critic. As you get closer to your 'real
life' yours will get more vocal and more cutting. The question is:
who is in charge? You, or that yappy voice inside your head?

Your inner critic might sound like it is speaking the truth but it
is just a scared puppy (a leftover part of your ancient lizard brain)
howling. So treat it gently. Here are three clues that it's your critic
speaking:

★ Look out for doomsday-style thinking such as 'if you do this
   stupid thing you will fail and everyone will laugh at you and
   you will end up living in a cardboard box'.

★ Take note when you speak to yourself the way you would
   not speak to a friend. Would you tell a friend: 'You don't
   have any strengths, don't be so big headed. You're doomed
   to stay stuck forever'? Of course not. So why is it okay to
   speak that way to yourself?

★ Look out for the words 'should' and 'should not' – they are
   your inner critic's favourite words.

What do you do when you spot your inner critic at work? Simple: realize he or she is not you. When you recognize that voice, just nod and say, 'oh yes, that's my inner critic'. Separate this voice from your conscious thoughts and soon you'll stop seeing these dooms-day thoughts as immutable fact, but as the mouthings of a scared ancient part of your brain. Some people like to give their critic a special name to reiterate it is not them.

Whatever you do don't fight against it: this puppy bites back with the most cutting words you can imagine. Your job isn't to kill it off, it's to calm it down, and work around it. Remember it oper-ates from a place of fear, so tell it it's okay, you're not going to die – you've just got one little project. Pat Top Dog on the head and send it back to sleep while you move on with your real life.

Remember, there's a big difference between the scary voice that says 'you'll never make it!' and reality. Part of your process is learn-ing to differentiate between the two.

EXERCISE   **Part 2 reflections – defining the dream**

Now it's time to pull together your thoughts from this section:

What are your favourite things that you came up with in the 'dreaming big' exercises in Chapters 3 and 4?

_____

_____

What did you notice in doing the internal GPS/defrosting process in Chapter 5?

_____

_____

How did you 'tailor' your free range career ideas (Chapter 6)? For example, did you choose a portfolio career, edit your ideas to create a bespoke solution, etc?

_____

_____

What strengths did you identify from th

_____

_____

What you are doing for your first P

_____

_____

And finally, tell me. What are:

The lessons from the book so to you back in school?

_____

_____

Your favourite free range ca

_____

_____

Your thoughts for where y

_____

_____

The questions you m

_____

_____

Congratulations! n
Now we move t
out good ideas y
perfectly matc s
   You are w s t
dream in th
with your p

PART 3
THINK
LIKE A FREE
RANGE
HUMAN

'Ok, now I have a few ideas but I don't really know if they will work or how to choose the right one!'

After going through 'dreaming big' in Part 2, some nagging questions might be coming up. You might be excited about these new possibilities but also thinking:

★ I have an idea of the life I want, but my ideas for getting *paid* are a bit vague.

★ Everything I think up needs too much investment to start.

★ I don't have the time to do another three-year degree to get qualified and my CV doesn't fit anything except what I'm doing now!

★ How do I know if this idea will really work?

Good news: almost everyone I have worked with thought one or more of those points was a barrier... before they learned another way, launched and broke free forever.

In this section, I introduce you to some out-of-the-box approaches Free Range Humans use to quickly figure out if ideas will work, choose the right idea, and wildly expand their options beyond their CV. Also, you'll learn how to start out for under £100.

If you already have one clear idea (or a portfolio) that you want to explore – great! Use this part of the book to refine it. If you are sitting with a few less clear thoughts, use the inspiration and approaches here to expand your options. At the end of this section you get a chance to define the idea you want to take forward, so please don't put pressure on yourself to start with the 'one perfect thing' here and now.

To get things going let's meet a real Free Range Human and see how he got started in an unusual way:

FREE RANGE PROFILE
PETER'S STORY – FROM
T-SHIRTS TO US$100K
WITHOUT AN OFFICE

Described as 'a spectacular example of what happens when you merge the power of pure creativity with ADHD and a dose of adventure', Peter Shankman is pretty successful these days.

Today, he is an entrepreneur, author and founder of companies such as HARO (Help a Reporter Out). In under a year, HARO went from a little Facebook group (which Peter started for free) to becoming the world's largest free resource for journalists looking for sources, drawing in advertising revenue of around US$1 million.[1] You could say that this man is doing well. But I'm not here to talk about his current business; what is most interesting is how he got started doing something very different.

When Peter decided to go free range back in 1998 he had no one bankrolling him, and no contacts. I spoke to Peter, and he shared the story of how he went from zero to his first major pay cheque:

> *It was the summer that* Titanic *was coming out on video. I figured there had to be someone else that hated that movie. So, on a whim, I had 500 T-shirts printed that said:* It Sank. Get Over It.
>
> *I went to* Times Square *with the T-shirts and I wound up selling the shirts in six hours. I made US$3,200 profit and that was my start-up money.*
>
> *After that, the story broke on* USA Today *and I wound up selling 10,000 shirts on the web at $15 a piece. I cleared about $100,000.*

Rewind a moment. *The story broke on* USA Today *and he made $100,000?* Here we were, thinking that $3,200 was a nice place to start. How did that happen? Did Peter have secret contacts? A qualification in T-shirt design? Peter shook his head when I asked him, and said:

> I had no media profile, I didn't know anyone, I just made the T-shirts because I thought it was funny and I went to Times Square and sold them. Then, I called a USA Today *lifestyle* reporter and said: 'I just did something really funny.'
>
> The reporter said, 'That's hysterical. Are you selling the shirts online now?', and I replied, 'Of course I am!' I wasn't, of course, so I had to then run off and build the worst website in the world and, the next thing I knew, the story ran and orders started coming in and that's how I made my first $100,000.

I love Peter's story for two reasons:

First, he did something *fast*. He took action before waiting to be noticed. Most people with that idea would just talk about it with their friends – '*hey it would be really funny if we printed that on a T-shirt!*' – but then they would probably find a heap of reasons why not to do it. A slightly more proactive person might get five printed and sell them to family.

Peter took something most people just talk about down the pub as a 'great idea' and he made it happen without overthinking – plus he shot for the top (Times Square, not your local mall!). Crucially, he didn't get hung up on whether he had enough experience or qualifications to make this happen. That's real free range action.

The second reason I love this story is that even after zipping up from 'the bottom' and selling his first T-shirts, Peter didn't settle for the middle. After his first six hours in Times Square he turned a tidy profit, knew he was on to something and already had a platform for success. He could have built slowly from there and been quite comfortable. But Peter took what he had and put it on speed and went straight to the top.

Now, I am not saying that if you go to Times Square and sell T-shirts and call reporters you're guaranteed to succeed! I am show-casing this story for the attitude: Peter didn't stop at the doubts that would hold most people back. He went from idea to execution in a few days without asking for permission.

It's not about waiting to be noticed, waiting for a big break or demanding to know exactly where it will end before starting. It's not about hiding your fabulousness under the excuse *If I'm good enough they will notice me.*

It's about making things happen even while others find reasons why not.

9 WHY YOU DON'T NEED AN ORIGINAL IDEA

'Ideas are in the air. There are lots of people thinking about – and probably working on – the same thing you are. And one of them is Google. Deal with it.'

Evan Williams, co-founder, Twitter

The 'originality' myth

'I have an idea but the problem is someone else is already doing it. My idea is too generic, the market is crowded. I'm probably too late.'

Someone 'stole' your idea? Back to the drawing board.

Myth buster

When I was getting started as a coach I stumbled across the website of someone who was offering exactly what I imagined for myself. Down to the design of her website she had created exactly my vision! Oh no, I thought. Someone's beat me to this idea. Worse, she had a big reputation and an established client base.

I almost gave up because my idea didn't seem original enough, but luckily I didn't, because a month into my new venture I realized I didn't want to be this 'competitor'. My priorities, message and who I wanted to work with were different from what I originally assumed. Had I let the discovery of her business stop me from starting mine I wouldn't be writing this for you today.

Originality isn't an idea you stumble on (that no one has thought of before), it's something you create by putting your own stamp on whatever you choose. But the catch is: originality comes when in motion.

When you discover someone doing the thing you want to do, ask yourself:

★ If you were magically handed their business right now, would you do things 100 per cent the same as they do?

★ Do they really have capacity to take on every single customer in this field?

★ Would they appeal to everyone you want to work with?

Think those through. Odds are there is more room for you than you imagine.

Free range third way

It would be safe to say that 'getting drunk and then filming yourself cooking on a home video' isn't the most genius job-escape strategy you've heard this century. It's also safe to say that you wouldn't be the first person to do that and then share it on YouTube. However, one of the most brilliant things I've seen this year has been someone doing just that.

One evening, Hannah Hart filmed a video on her Mac of herself cooking while drinking wine in her sister's kitchen. She was cooking grilled cheese but forgot the cheese, which tells you everything you need to know.

Hannah posted this video on YouTube to share it with just one friend. She called it My Drunk Kitchen. Within a few months she had more than 100,000 fans. She now has more than 25 million video views. In fact, I urge you to hit pause on this book and look up her website in order to get the full effect: **www.hartoandco.com/my-drunk-kitchen**

Now, back to the point. Hannah's idea in its raw form was somewhat questionable. Can you imagine telling your friends: '*I have a great idea. I'm going to drink a whole bottle of red wine and cook stuff I don't have ingredients for, and then post it online and get famous! Plus I can't cook.*'

That's hardly a brilliant idea. It certainly wasn't brand new. (There are dozens of other drunk cooking attempts on YouTube, pre-dating Hannah's first video. None of them had high views.) However, judging from her reviews and appearances in *Time* magazine, on *CBS News* and many others places, Hannah's execution of this idea is catching people's attention. I can pretty much guarantee that had Hannah sat in a room evaluating the feasibility of this not-so-original idea then she wouldn't be where she is today.

That exposure (along with YouTube advertising revenue) allowed Hannah to quit her office job and pursue her love of making people laugh.

John D Gartner, a psychiatry professor who writes on the psychology of entrepreneurs, points out that 'great entrepreneurs often do not create original ideas – they grasp the significance of an idea, wherever it comes from, and leap on it with everything they have.'[2] In other words, sometimes the best ideas sound less than promising at first and only become brilliant in the execution.

Today, you are lucky enough to be able to get an idea out into the world, for free, in a very short period of time. Use this as your platform for trying out your idea and making it original and uniquely you.

Four ways to get original (by being more you):

1. Put your stamp on it

For every person who comes up with a unique widget that goes viral, there are hundreds making a great free range living as consultants, coaches and interior designers. What matters is putting your own personal stamp on what you do.

What could you do to tweak an existing idea to be more you? This could be how you present it, how you deliver it and who you offer it to (ie could you tailor it exclusively for a specific group of people you know something about?). Instead of looking 'out there' for originality, create it yourself by putting your stamp on something that's already working.

2. Obvious to you, amazing to others

This is one for people giving advice or offering guidance.

Ever felt that everything you think of has been said before? That is a common fear. However, I am betting not every idea in your favourite books was original (ie never said at any time since Plato to today). Imagine if all your favourite authors had refused to publish because *that has already been said.*

As Derek Sivers, founder of CD Baby, points out, we don't all think the same. What seems obvious to you is wildly original to someone else. He is right. I am lucky enough to hang out with some wonderful writers and thinkers, people who others hold up as examples of true originality, yet almost all of these people see their own words as nothing new. *For a fun illustration watch Sivers's short animation on originality:* **http://frh.me/originalsivers**

The truth is that we all receive messages in different ways at different times, and most of us need to hear several people's interpretations before one hits home. So don't shy back from adding to a message you believe in. What would you say if you didn't think it was too obvious?

3. Notice connections

The iPod felt so very exciting when it launched – especially the handy little clickwheel interface. But how original was it?

Bill Fischer and Andy Boynton in their book *The Idea Hunter* point out that the iPod clickwheel was not created by technologists but discovered by an Apple marketing guy, Phil Schiller and his team, who found it on a 1983 Hewlett Packard workstation: 'Schiller bridged the distance between one product and another that he was trying to improve,' they explain. 'The click wheel was an old idea, waiting to be dusted off and put to some other use. It wasn't an invention.'[3]

If you want to get more original, get curious. Notice what is around you, read books that others in your field don't read, fill yourself up with inspiration and get in the habit of making connections between unrelated ideas in your everyday life. This is a killer way to create an idea that is uniquely yours.

4. Discover your difference

Want to be original? It's not just about an original idea, it's about original communication. So don't copy someone else's style: develop your own. Discover your uniqueness by getting into motion. A simple place to start is to open a free blog on **www.blogger.com** or **www.wordpress.com,** and write your message like no one is watching (and hey, if it's a new blog then they probably aren't). Write twice a week and hit publish no matter what. If you are not a writer, then video or audio-record your message. However you do it, this process is one of the best ways to clarify your thoughts. You may start out sounding like someone else, but as you hit publish more and more you'll start to discover a message and words that are uniquely yours.

Above all, remember that any 'good market' will be crowded already, and if it's empty, it won't stay that way for long. You will have competition no matter what... *and that's a good thing.* It's to your benefit that someone else was the trailblazer: much easier to sell something when people actually understand what it is because other people have done the hard slog of raising awareness!

If you're really worried about competition, rest assured: using the techniques in this book (in particular Chapter 22) you'll learn how to stand out from the crowd no matter what. But for now, know that avoiding the crowd is not a long-term solution and it's definitely not a reason to back away from an idea you're attracted to.

10 WHY YOU DON'T NEED OODLES OF EXPERIENCE
(what you have to offer other than your CV)

'It's never too late to be who you might have been.'

George Eliot

The 'oodles of experience' myth

'So many people are already doing this and they have years of experience. Why would anyone pay me? Maybe I should get another degree first.'

Myth buster

If you've had ideas but felt trapped by your CV, you're going to love this. Outside of the career cage no one gives you money for years' of experience or qualifications. With no job interviews to pass, the CV is no longer king, and oodles of experience is not necessarily a golden ticket to a great income.

I mean it: I have people come to me with 10 years' experience (and a Master's degree in the topic) who are earning less than people with two years' experience (and a load of passion). In Part 4 you will learn how to avoid their mistakes and stand out big-time, but for now, I want to show you what is possible with what you have.

How to become a wedding videographer (without an expensive camera or attending film school)

Run a search on how to start out as a wedding videographer and the advice generally goes: invest in a top-end camera (costly), do a video-editing course (long), post ads in your local paper (and hope you stand out from the other hundred videographers in your area). Yawn.

Daisy Jenks did things differently. She grabbed a hand-held camera, started filming and then turned her videos into a fun home-made musical. Think *Glee* with a wedding theme. Here's how it works:

> *The client picks a song and I go around their event with a lyrics sheet and a little camera. I go up to guests and ask them to do a line of a song and a dance routine, then I come back and edit them into a music video.*

In Daisy's videos, wedding guests become the lip-synching and dancing stars; everything – from the bride getting ready to the guests dancing into the night – becomes part of a short piece that blows traditional videos out of the water.

> *I have been picking up a camera and filming for as long as I can remember. It used to be just a bit of fun with my sister, but one year I started out filming families at a resort in Greece and then stitching it together in time to music. At the end of the holiday I showed the video and they all loved it.*
>
> *By the time I got back to the UK, a friend asked me to do a wedding – I only had a laptop so I filmed everything on that! Then I got a little hand-held Panasonic HD camera and got asked to do a 21st birthday.*
>
> *It all went from there. I got work through a mix of word of mouth, people seeing my YouTube videos, online, and the events companies I partner with. I've done weddings, corporate events, birthdays, and the work keeps growing. I just love making music videos and being part of people's events.*[4]

Free range third way

What you don't ask is as important as what you do ask

Daisy didn't ask 'how is a wedding video supposed to look?' That means she ended up different from the crowd. Starting without a rulebook is the antithesis of the old career-cage approach that says: 'We can't take a risk: if something goes wrong we'll get in trouble and miss out on that promotion.'

Out in free range land, there is no prize for staying safe. Given you can start out without risking your money, there is no reason not to explore ideas that are different from the norm. Amazing results come from getting creative, pushing the boundaries, daring to be different.

Stop comparing your inside to other people's outside

Ever been researching an idea, hit the website of someone who is already out there doing it, read their 'about' page... and immediately felt your heart sink? That person has so much more experience and status than you, how could you compete? Well here's a good first step: *stop reading other people's 'about' pages*.

The 'about' page is not an unbiased biography. It is a piece of writing created with the explicit intent of convincing the reader that the person is a perfect fit for this work. So you are unlikely to hit the website of a freelance events organizer and read:

> *Laura used to work as an accountant and the only way she became an events organizer was by blagging it for the first three events, claiming she organized her company's internal events (which really meant she set up last year's department Christmas party, where wine was served in plastic cups).*
>
> *Her degree has nothing to do with her business. Actually, neither does the bulk of her professional experience. But, you know, hire her.*

No, you're not likely to read that, even if it is true (which it possibly is). So save yourself the heartache and stop comparing your warts-and-all reality with other people's highlights reel.

Embrace the outsider advantage

Instead of thinking about what you do not have – or what you are 'throwing away' – consider what you do have. For example, Emma Reynolds (case study opposite) went from a career in marketing to launching a successful HR consultancy, yet Emma says her non-traditional background has been an advantage in this competitive field:

> *We don't sound like everyone else – that's because we are not. That has been our biggest strength.*
>
> *We look at HR from a marketing perspective. The questions we ask are normal in my old field but new in HR. Our fresh perspective is part of why we are winning contracts away from the world's biggest consultancies. That outsider clarity has been a real advantage.*[5]

In another example, Dan Cobley, director of marketing for Google, brings unique insights to his work via his physics background.[6] In short, when you are free range everything about your life counts; nothing is thrown away. The very things that make you different might well be your edge.

MINI CASE STUDY

The first thing you need to know about me is that I have the words *carpe diem* tatooed on my foot. The second thing is that I don't have a university degree; I dropped out twice.

I had an idea for my first business when I was on an overseas business trip. My colleague and I jotted down our idea on a piece of paper on the flight home, we touched down, and both resigned the next day. Having quit so fast we needed quick cash for our salaries so we took out a small car loan – there was no car, we just used it to get going! All we needed were a website and a few business cards, and we set up both in our one month notice period. We got our first client within two weeks, paid off the loan in the first few months and from that point we were self-funded and everything took off from there.

For my next business I moved from London to Hong Kong, because I thought it would be interesting. I started by myself this time, created my own website and got going for under £500. I didn't know anyone in Hong Kong but I simply went out and met people. Soon I met my co-director, Jared, and we just got out and got clients.

We were profitable from day one and have been ever since: we will never rent expensive office space and we're very much free range! This gives us the freedom to experiment. Our company's philosophy is Work Sucks (meaning most people's experience of it sucks because of the way work has been traditionally designed). Our mission is to change all that. We are working with companies such as AXA and Nestlé, flying all over Asia, and even running our first TedX event this year!

I live in an amazing city, in an incredible part of the world, and I love what I do. Every day I wake up, look in the mirror and say 'let's carpe the f*ck out of this diem'. This is *fun*.

Emma Reynolds, Hong Kong, **www.e3reloaded.com**

Think beyond your job title

One of my favourite cartoonists, Scott Adams (creator of the 'Dilbert' comic strips) says:

> *The first thing you should learn... is how to make yourself valuable...*
>
> *I succeeded as a cartoonist with negligible art talent, some basic writing skills, an ordinary sense of humor and a bit of experience in the business world. The 'Dilbert' comic is a combination of all four skills. The world has plenty of better artists, smarter writers, funnier humorists and more experienced business people. The rare part is that each of those modest skills is collected in one person. That's how value is created.*[7]

Experience is not the same as a job title. If there is something in your work or life that you a) enjoy and b) are good at, then *no matter how small it may seem right now*, that will be able to be translated into something else of value. Combine a few of these, and that's the start of a great free range career. The first step is to identify what you have to offer beyond your obvious CV.

For example, Robert Watson had a corporate life that started in engineering and ended in HR. As an engineer Robert was an excellent logical thinker: 'my natural style is seeing things as a flow-chart,' he explains. Then when Robert moved into HR he learned how people think, and also how to communicate his direct feed-back in a way that more creative types will understand. So when Robert went free range he combined that experience and set himself up as a coach and editor for authors – a role that includes being the freelance editor of this book! He now uses his engineer-style approach – detailed and specific – to help wordy authors (ahem) distil their message and ensure readability.

Book editing is not a 'transferable skill' you would find on Robert's CV – he had to look at what he was good at and enjoyed (beyond a job title) to identify this hidden value. When you look beyond your CV or traditional 'transferable skills' then you will have something of value to offer.

If you are struggling to think of examples in your own life, consider what people come to you for help with already, and what they value about you. For example, while in his job Robert was confused as to why people came to him – an engineer – for help with workplace conflict and life advice. So he asked and one person replied, 'I like that you see things so logically and don't let me get bogged down in the emotions.' That was the first time Robert realized his engineering approach could be a valuable advantage in other areas of life.

To help you identify what you have to offer, let's delve into your advantage case.

EXERCISE   Unlock your Advantage Case

It's time to give yourself credit for what you have learned, discovered and gathered in your life to date.

In this exercise you are writing down a 'contents list' of your Advantage Case – a virtual case packed with your hidden assets that you can take with you wherever you go on your free range journey. To give you some idea of the sorts of things that others identified in this exercise, some recent answers include:

* my ability to learn fast;
* a ready-made virtual office (that beautiful local café where I often see people work with laptops);
* being able to Google the answer to just about any question!
* an NLP practitioner certification;
* skill of finding the root cause of any problem (ie honing in on what really needs to be done);
* a supportive partner who wants me to be happy;
* skills at creating beautifully presented documents;
* my love of, and years of practice at, writing compelling stories;
* excellent organizer and planner (from years of writing and delivering lesson plans as a teacher!);
* the experience of being well travelled and good at meeting new people.

▶

◀

Now it's your turn. To help you unlock your hidden advantages, write down four of your own assets under each of the headings below:

Career history (think beneath the official job description and list out the parts where you feel you shine, and the things that you've loved to do):

_____

_____

Study, things you've done on the side:

_____

_____

Life experience:

_____

_____

Personal life (supportive friends, freedom, finances, etc):

_____

_____

Personal traits and strengths:

_____

_____

Congratulations! You now have 20 advantages, and this is just the beginning. You can extend your list as you go on. Later, in Chapter 25 (Instant Status) we are going to build on these to get you that positive perception that can take you from zero to must-have person in a short timeframe.

TIP   **Check yourself for Impostor Syndrome**

Do you find yourself easily dismissing praise for your own advantages or successes? Do you instead focus on the reasons you're not quite good enough? If so, you might be experiencing Impostor Syndrome.

Valerie Young writes about Impostor Syndrome, a mindset that means many people secretly worry about getting 'found out' for not being as smart or good as people seem to believe they are. Valerie explained to me:

> If you identify with the so-called impostor syndrome, then it's going to be harder for you to see your own accomplishments through the same lens as you see those of others. That's because despite evidence to the contrary... you've become masterful at explaining away, minimizing, and discounting these indicators of your success with words like... It was dumb luck... The stars were aligned... oh the judges just liked me.
>
> What you see far more clearly are the gaps in knowledge or experience, the stuff you've yet to accomplish. But it's a huge set-up. It's as if you're using a trick scale on which only negative evidence counts.

In her book *The Secret Thoughts of Successful Women* (2011) Valerie points out that people who experience Impostor Syndrome sometimes also put pressure on themselves to be perfect almost immediately – an impossibly high bar. As she says: 'remember that your first draft, first presentation, first painting, or first anything is never going to be as good as your second – or your two hundredth'.

In other words, don't use the fact that you're not world class in two hours as an excuse not to keep going.

11 WHAT A FREE RANGE BUSINESS LOOKS LIKE
(or: what can I do other than start a café?)

'I've heard someone say that our problems aren't the problem; it's our solutions that are the problem.'

Anne Lamott

In the last few chapters we have learnt why you don't need an original idea, why you don't need 10 years' experience or a PhD in the topic, and how you can start now. All of which have hopefully opened up a few more options for you. The aim of this chapter is to open up even more avenues by showing you the main types of things successful free rangers *actually* do for a living... which tends to be a bit different from what most people expect.

You see, the most common ideas I hear from people who want to quit their jobs are 'start a café/book shop/B&B'.

The problem with those solutions is that they are a bit rubbish. (Sorry, was I supposed to be subtle about that? Oops.)

Okay, I'm exaggerating a little. There's nothing wrong with these dreams. In fact I used to fantasize about starting a café until I realized that actually the life of a café owner is a lot of hard work cleaning, checking stock and triple-checking details, which is far from my vision of sitting around having interesting conversations and spending time languidly redecorating a beautiful space. Did I mention you were stuck in one place every day as well?

You see, when I speak to people with these sorts of dreams, it turns out that 90 per cent of the time they don't really want to start that café or B&B, *they want the life that they imagine comes with it.* The problem is, their idea-sphere for getting that life is currently limited.

If you've spent your life on the career-cage path, it's natural that your ideas about what you can do instead revolve around services you currently use (or shops you see on your local high street). That does not make those ideas your only options.

None of the above ideas are natural free range businesses. They all require start-up capital and are hard to experiment with on the side. Also, do the maths: it's darn hard to make good money from them. One of the reasons for this is outgoing costs. Most businesses that fail go under because of premises or other outgoing costs, which is exactly what free range businesses avoid.

However, if such an idea has been your lifelong dream, then go for it! I don't want to stop anyone doing their One Big Dream... but if this is just one 'maybe' on a list of many ideas then the point I'm making is that there are a lot of other options that might be better suited to getting the life you are looking for.

Here are some alternatives: the four free range business types.

Four free range business types (plus one extra option)

1. Services

Services include giving advice, providing support, or doing an actual task – essentially, anything where you *get paid for your time*. For example, web designer, therapist, relationship coach, speaker, virtual assistant, accountant, freelance writer, consultant or organic gardener.

Verdict for full-time free range freedom

Doing something and getting paid for it is the simplest sort of business to start. When you are paid for your time all you need in order to start is to have a service to offer and be willing to offer it: there is no barrier to putting yourself out there. This means 'service' type ideas are a great starting point for your first free range venture.

The downside of selling your time is that, well, you are timebound. How many clients can you take on in one month? Multiply that number by your rates and that's your earning limit. However, if you get creative with how you package your services, you can make services earn far more, with a better and more secure lifestyle, than the norm. Here is one way of earning more for your time:

TIP **Up your hourly rate**

Supercharge your earning power by not charging per hour. Instead of saying 'I charge £50 per hour for image consulting' present your 'Style Springclean pack' and include a fixed number of consulting sessions (with clear outcomes for each), prepatory worksheets for the client, and some recorded interviews with people who have been through this process, sharing how they made sure their style changes lasted in their busy lives. You'll have an easier time selling this package for £300+ than you would selling six hours of individual consulting at £50 an hour!

Another idea is to deliver what you do in a group setting in order to make the most of your time. For example, if instead of taking on one individual at a time, you work with a group of 10 people at once, you can earn 10 times as much for the same amount of time (if you keep the price the same) or 5 times more (if you halve the price compared to individual treatment). Of course, only do this if you enjoy a group environment!

However you do it, when you package up what you do and get away from an hourly rate, you escape the price-comparison game, and your earnings go up. Plus it's a great opportunity to get creative with what you do.

If you choose this option be sure to check out the Part 4 chapters on creating a consistent income without paying for advertising.

---

2. Virtual products

A virtual product is one that costs you nothing to make and that can be sold and downloaded online automatically (eg an e-guide or e-book). It typically contains information (or motivation) and can include words, audio, video: any medium you choose to deliver the information *without* your presence.

Examples

Benny Lewis's language-learning e-guide is a perfect example. I also create virtual products as part of my free range portfolio, and it is this addition that has allowed me to help many people break free over the past few years (while also allowing me to travel the world).

Here's how a virtual product works: let's say you have an idea to teach public speaking to beginners. You love the idea in theory but you know it will mean you only get paid for the hours you work (and that doesn't suit the flexible lifestyle you want). Solution: turn that idea into a virtual product.

Make a list of the 10 steps you would take people through when helping them become confident speakers. Then, jot down the parts of your teaching where most people go 'wow, that made such a difference!' Now create a guide called *10 Steps to Fearless Public Speaking*, and offer that as a downloadable course. You are now helping people and earning money independently of your time.

Of course, you can still run the live speaking training if you're excited about that, but you have the security of the virtual product helping you keep a steady income in between sessions. Alternatively, like Benny, you could make this guide your main income.

A few variations: if you don't want to sell your own product, you can get paid a percentage by promoting someone else's (as an 'affiliate'). Alternatively, a virtual product can also take the form of community for which you sell membership. The possibilities are endless!

Verdict for full-time free range freedom

Virtual products are a strong option that can give that magic balance of good earnings, flexibility and time freedom. All you require is your time, your brain, and an understanding of what your clients want and you can create a virtual product. Once your product is out there, it can make money over and over. Make it once, and it can help people again and again no matter what you are doing.

How much can this earn? Well, common wisdom says you can't make a full-time living off a £10 e-book. And unless you have unusually high website traffic, common wisdom would be right. That's why e-guides, and full online courses, cost more than £10.

Do-it-yourself online courses sell from at the low end £47, and at the top end *thousands*. What you can charge depends on the value you put in, and how well it's tailored and presented to a specific audience.

Do the sums: if you sell an average of one a day at £97 that's around £3,000 per month. Plus, if you get creative and add in an element of interaction with you, such as a session to ask any questions and get personal help, then you can easily raise the price. Or, if you get into it, you can create several virtual offerings and the sky is the limit income-wise.

So watch out for that girl in the café tapping away at her laptop: you might think she's scraping a living with a little hobby, but she might be part of the new free range generation and earning more than you imagine.

Now, I'd be doing you a disservice if I pretended that sticking up an e-guide will make you an instant living. You do have to put in work, and it genuinely has to be good stuff that you care about. You also have to put in the time to build trust and gather your audience (that's what I'll help you do in Part 4).

> **HINT**   to ensure quality make sure you have helped people with this topic in the real world before creating a virtual product. So if you have the idea for public speaking training, your first port of call should not be to make an e-course, your first step is to actually work with people (as discussed on the Play Project pages!). Then use what you learn from that to create a meaningful product.

3. Advertising

Create content on a website, bring in traffic, then sell advertising space to people who want to communicate with the people who are visiting your content. For example, if you create a YouTube channel you can become a YouTube partner and earn from the ads they place on your page.

Examples

Emma and Ollie make their living from their YouTube channel, My Vox Songs, which shares their nursery rhyme animations. A world away from their former corporate jobs, their new life was made possible primarily because of revenue from the advertising YouTube places on their channel.

BONUS

Read the story of how Emma taught herself animation (in the evenings) and built up My Vox Songs from a personal project, created to entertain her son, into a full-time living supporting herself and her family in London. **http://frh.me/emmaandollie** To go straight to Emma's story, scan the QR code with your smartphone or tablet.

Dom and Rob had the idea for the Escape the City website while in their cubicle jobs; they started with just a free Wordpress blog and today they are (full-time) running a 65,000-strong international community of people looking for opportunities outside the traditional corporate mainstream. Dom and Rob make their income primarily from revenue from the hand-picked job ads displayed to the community.

Verdict for full-time free range freedom

Advertising is tempting but often misunderstood. With the exception of YouTube, signing up to a website advertising programme and whacking up ads, hoping to get paid based on traffic, will not make you anywhere near a full-time living (think of it more as coffee-money). Indeed, most full-time bloggers don't make their living from this sort of advertising (they tend to make the bulk of their income from virtual products sold off their website, or from consulting/speaking gained off the back of their blog).

The people (such as Dom and Rob) who do well with the advertising model tend to sell their own advertising space by 1) building a loyal following, and 2) doing deals with hand-picked advertising clients.

4. Physical products

Essentially, making and selling stuff. From hand-woven dog beds to art to market-stall food.

Examples

A typical example is Rachel Winard, who you will meet in Chapter 23. A former attorney, Rachel now makes a full-time living by selling hand-made soap in her online shop. There are also some inspiring examples of free rangers who integrate their love of travel with their business idea (such as Petra Barran who created the ChocStar van and travelled across the country selling chocolate goodies at festivals and markets).[8]

Verdict for full-time free range freedom

It depends how you set this up. Keep in mind that if you have to make as well as sell your goods (and buy the ingredients/equipment) you might have to put quite a bit more time in to get the return you want. For this reason I recommend that you only choose physical products if you know, deep down, that this is what you really want to do and are determined to put in the time and make it happen. Why? Because if this is your biggest passion, then the time you put into making the product won't feel like work.

5. Mix it up

It is likely that a few of these approaches appeal to you. Simple solution: mix it up. This is how many free rangers create a great income and lifestyle filled with variety.

For example, Connie Hozvicka quit her job to run Dirty Footprints Studios, an inspiring online space and blog, where she helps people create Fearless (intuitive) art. As part of Dirty Footprints, Connie offers virtual products (such as a pre-recorded online video workshop), services (live art courses, run either as online adventures or as live desert retreats), and at one stage she included physical products (selling her own art). Each of these strands alone could have been enough to make Connie a nice full-time living, but by mixing it up Connie creates more variety and vibrancy in her day, allowing her to get paid for her loves of teaching, writing and creating art.

MINI CASE STUDY

I used to be a school principal. Then, in my thirties, I quit my job and created a life where I can be wherever I want, whenever I want. Now I teach an online-college class, coach virtually via Skype, and recently became a Zumba instructor. For the past two years, I have lived in South America, Central America, Australia, South-East Asia and the Pacific Islands. I return to the Midwest in the summers and drive around in my '99 convertible, visiting friends and family.

This fall, I will attend a writing festival in Bali, interview social entrepreneurs for a book I'm writing, volunteer at a girls' school in Cambodia, catch up with friends, chase the sun and check out Myanmar.

Kristi Hemmer, Iowa, USA

What works for you?

Which models did you find most attractive? How could you use them? What else do you need to know? Gather your thoughts by filling in the table below (there is room for more than one favourite in case you want to Mix It Up!). Write your answers below:

Model I found attractive	What I could offer	How this fits the life I want	I would like to know more about
eg virtual products	eg do-it-yourself dog-training pack	eg gives me the option to travel	eg where to find the audience for this product

12 HOW TO FREE RANGE-IFY YOUR IDEA

Now you know some ways that Free Range Humans make a living, how do your ideas fit? If your income-generating idea in its current form isn't *quite* free range enough to experiment with and get going with what you have now, help is at hand. It's time to free range-ify your idea.

The secret to free range-ifying an idea is to figure out which part of it really gets you fired up, and find another way to do that. Here's an example of someone who did just that:

Charlie Haynes runs Urban Writers' Retreats in London. Currently her one-day retreats run both live and online, she has been featured in national press such as *The Guardian*. Sounds idyllic, right?

However this wasn't the business Charlie meant to start. She wanted to create a writers' workspace, a place where members could go and work any time and host events. But she couldn't afford the rent and all of the equipment, plus having to deal with all of those overheads sounded daunting when she wasn't sure if it would work.

Charlie explains what happened next:

I was on the bus on my way to work one morning and had been mulling over my exercise procrastination issues. I was contemplating doing a fitness bootcamp, and it just hit me that all of the things I wanted to get from the fitness bootcamp – companionship and being forced to get on with exercising and actually making visible progress – were the same things I wanted for myself from a writers' workspace.

I thought: if a fitness bootcamp would be better than trying to run by myself every day (and not doing it), wouldn't a writing bootcamp work the same way?

So I set up a free website and found the cheapest venue I could hire that had the bare minimum requirements and asked for guinea pigs, charging just enough to cover the costs. I ran the event, then asked people to fill in a feedback form and make suggestions before they left, and then I made changes the next time around.

When it was clear that I could make money from this, and people got a lot done, I decided it was worth investing in web hosting and hiring a better venue. I learned how to build my website and how to do all the social media stuff, newsletters, etc, myself. That meant it only cost a couple of hundred quid to get going, which you can save by not going on big nights out for a month or so while you work on getting set up.

Now, with the network I've built up, I can do other things such as online courses that are very cheap to run from anywhere in the world.

Had Charlie sat with her original idea of a permanent writers' workspace she would possibly have never started. By the way, if you're thinking 'she must be so brave to just dive in and get started!' Charlie would like to say:

Even without the money issue, starting was scary! Just making phone calls to potential venues was hard, but once I'd made a few steps it was easier to keep up the momentum.

You can do this.

13 HOW TO START FOR UNDER £100

In this guide, I'll share the resources you need to start for under £100. This is not about being tight or looking cheap. *This is about how to get champagne results on a cava budget by knowing what to look for and where to get it.*

The truth is that when you look at what people spend their money on in their first year, about 20 per cent of their spending gets them 80 per cent of their results. That other 80 per cent of spending? Expensive fluff. When you know what works, and what doesn't, you can hone and get fabulous results without spending a fortune. Here's how I discovered this for myself.

The £100,000 question

A few weeks after I started on my free range venture, I was sitting in a café thinking, 'I wish someone would hand me £100,000 so I could get the word out about what I do!' I'd been thinking this a lot, and that day I realized I'd never articulated what I'd do with that hypothetical 'free money'.

So I opened up a new document and wrote out my wish list. On the list were things like 'big ads in magazines' and 'a really great website' and 'membership of clubs where I can meet people doing similar things'. Then, I wrote out why I wanted each of those things.

That's when I saw it: I could have it all. How? By focusing on the *outcome* rather than the wrapping.

What I wanted	Why I wanted it	What outcome I wanted
advertising	people would hear about me	get clients easily and consistently
website	respect and interest	get the right sort of clients easily and consistently
membership of clubs	partnerships	have fun working with others (and get clients easily and consistently)

Next I looked at how likely it was that these wishes would get me that outcome.

Would advertising get me enough exposure to get clients 'easily and consistently'? As I knew from my previous work in marketing consultancy and advertising analysis, the answer was 'probably not'. I figured I'd get a boost from some ads, but it wouldn't last forever.

Would a better website get me respect from potential clients and raise interest? Maybe... provided I had enough traffic (which I didn't). Would a nice website *really* convert visitors to clients? That wasn't so certain. I started to realize that the websites I was 'stalking' because I coveted their beautiful design were not websites at which I was spending any money.

Okay, maybe the ideas I had for what I needed were a bit off the mark. So the question turned to: is spending that money the only way to get those results? No way! Suddenly something switched on in my head: here's what I did.

Get champagne results on a cava budget

To discover what matters, go back to first principles. Always ask *why* you need what you think you need.

This is what I did. First, website. Instead of sulking about not having a top-of-the-line website, I invested instead in *learning* exactly what does and does not work for a website in my field. Where 'work' means bringing in the right sort of clients consistently and easily.

To my surprise, the sites that worked were not the sort of slick Flash-heavy website I was coveting. As a result, I created a website by myself with no technical knowledge (using the resources I share in the £100 starter pack below). This website is still earning me money to this day – in fact it gets a better return than any of the sites I wished I'd had in my early days. That was my first discovery: that investment in my own knowledge could pay off many times over.

Another thing I was lacking was connections. I was outside all the circles of interesting conversations, and didn't know any other creative business people. So, instead of shelling out £1,000 a year per club membership, I started emailing the type of people I wanted to meet, and meeting with them for coffee. No agenda, no pushing, just interested in meeting them and what I could do for *them*. Not everyone said *yes*, but some did, and that was my chance to get started.

Because I wasn't able to just throw money at the problem, I was forced to really consider what did and did not work. That simple process got me better results than randomly throwing £100,000 at the problem ever would have!

This story ends with a twist: not long after doing this exercise I received an unexpected small inheritance. Nothing near £100,000, alas, but enough that it meant something to me. A few months before, I would have thrown the cash at my business. Yet now, I sat back, looked at the options and realized I didn't need to spend it. There was nothing it could generate that I couldn't do myself.

To this date I have never spent any of that money on my businesses. Instead I learnt a valuable lesson: there are some big benefits to starting small.

MINI CASE STUDY

At first, I was convinced I did not have the technical skills to develop my own website. However, these resources, and the free range approach of breaking things down into simple steps, means that I now have a website that many people assume I've paid a company to do (and they are so impressed when I tell them I did it myself!).

Gina Musa, London, UK

BONUS AUDIO

Three big benefits of starting small

In this four-minute audio learn three simple reasons you can get a huge advantage by NOT spending thousands of pounds to get started. **http://frh.me/bigsmallbenefits** To go straight to this audio, scan the QR code with your smartphone or tablet.

So what might *you* need to get started? To give this information the space it deserves, I've created a free bonus downloadable resource guide on starting for under £100.

BONUS

Free range resource pack (what you *really* need to start a business for under £100)

In this pack you will find:

* ★ insider knowledge on the tools you need to start a website and blog;
* ★ quality design on a budget;
* ★ easy ways to take online payments;
* ★ tips on hosting an event without a big location budget;
* ★ how to find a virtual assistant to take on the parts of your work that don't play to your strengths;
* ★ a 'dummie's' guide to insurance;
* ★ what you do and don't need for business registration and tax;
* ★ how to start a mailing list;
* ★ tips for finding fabulous free range workspaces.

Using this bonus guide you can experiment and start now with the money you have, and save any extra cash for the things that really matter, such as learning how to build and expand your business, or investing in one-offs that will make a real difference.

Get the bonus free range 'Start For Under £100' resource pack here: **http://www.free-range-humans.com/resourcepack**
To go straight to this Free Range Resource Pack, scan the QR code with your smartphone or tablet.

NOTE This pack is the only place in this book where we discuss business registration, tax or insurance. This is a conscious choice: I don't want to perpetuate the myth that these topics are the most time consuming or difficult part of starting as your own boss when, in fact, the opposite is true (in the UK). It is almost certainly faster and simpler than you think so don't let fear of paperwork hold you back: take action now, starting with the resource pack.

DOS AND DON'TS   **Dos and don'ts of starting on a shoestring**

DO make sure you have the basics: a laptop, a mobile phone (ideally a smartphone for ultimate email portability). Put together, both of these will cover 90 per cent of your needs; for example I use my iPhone for blog photos and my laptop's inbuilt camera for the videos.

DON'T assume you need top-of-the-range kit to get started. Always ask 'can I do without this?' before buying. For example, I ran my whole business off a bottom-end netbook (small laptop) for more than a year. I set myself a goal of what I wanted to reach before buying my shiny Macbook, which made it a far more meaningful purchase.

DO get creative with free range options. For example, did you know that you can use Skype as a regular telephone? Instead of installing an extra line as a private 'work phone number', you can buy a telephone number on Skype.com. This number looks like a normal landline number based in your home town. When someone calls it they are charged regular local rates and they have no idea they are calling a computer. Plus, you can call from and pick up this number no matter where you are in the world, so long as you have an Internet connection.

DO have taste. Starting small should never mean looking cheap. So:

DON'T use a free business card service where the cards are a) printed on flimsy paper, or b) include the name of the printing company on the back. This says, 'I don't believe in what I do enough to spend £10 on it.' Not cool.

DO use moo.com for affordable and awesome business cards. The designs are simple to create, look fabulous and are surprisingly affordable. Hint: start out with a small number of cards in case you change your mind about the name or design.

DON'T lose £100 to save £5. Is a saving taking up your time, mental space and stopping you moving forward? If so, that's not a saving, that's a cost.

DO invest in yourself: the best free rangers are constantly learning. Investing in your own education reaps rewards over and over.

14 HOW TO KNOW IF YOUR IDEA WILL WORK
(test your idea in seven days)

**'You don't have to be great to start,
but you have to start to be great.'** *Joe Sabah*

Let's recap what we've covered over the last few chapters: we've discovered that you don't need a wildly original idea, you don't need 20 years' experience, and you can get started for under £100. Rocking. However, a big question tends to come up right around now: *is your idea really going to work?*

Figuring out if an idea is viable isn't exactly rocket science. You need two things: 1) people who want to pay for it; 2) the potential for it to pay enough to reach the income you want.

That's what it boils down to. Are people keen to pay for it? Can you make it pay enough to suit your needs?

Let's deal with these separately, starting with the latter.

How to know if your idea can pay enough

I once received an email from someone who was trying to make a living from hand-made envelopes. She had been making and selling her beautiful envelopes for years but never quite got it off the ground enough to cover her City-lawyer salary, and two mortgages. When I asked what had been holding her back she immediately replied, 'Time. I'm so busy, but I know if I find time to make more envelopes then things will work out.'

Hmm. Something didn't add up here (and I mean that literally).

Five minutes and one calculator later it was crystal clear that in order to make her bare minimum she would have to sell more than

80 envelopes a day. That's about 2,500 a month. Can you imagine trying to find 80 people a day to buy envelopes (let alone finding the time to make them by hand?)

When I pointed out the numbers she was floored. Somehow, this highly intelligent person had never, in three years, stopped to do a five-minute calculation. Discovering the truth meant she was able to focus on making another more profitable idea work as her escape-vessel, and continued the envelopes on the side as a secondary income stream.

Moral of the story: calculators can be cool, kiddies. Here's how to do this for yourself right now.

Identify how much you need to make per month (very roughly). Now divide that by how much you expect to make from your main product. So if you need to make £4,000 (before tax) and your main product/service is £400 then £4,000 divided by £400 = 10 sales per month.

That's little more than two sales a week. Now imagine you are launched, and have been out there doing this for a while, and people are interested in what you have to offer. In that scenario, does two per week (or whatever your number may be) sound like a reasonable number to achieve? If so, congratulations! You have an idea worth exploring further.

HINT   don't get bogged down in finding exact numbers. This is a sanity check not a plan. Do this now.

TIP   If you realize the idea as it stands isn't going to support you no matter how successful you get, either adapt the idea (eg raise the price or find another sort of buyer who can pay/buy more) or add in extra income streams (eg create those greeting cards as part of a wider portfolio). It doesn't mean you won't end up using that idea at some point, it simply means it might not be your fastest way out of your job right now.

How to know if people will really pay for what you have to offer

Now you know your idea can earn enough in theory, the next step is to discover whether people are willing to pay for it in practice.

The best way of finding out if people are likely to pay is to run the two free range 'pay tests' below. The first pay test you can do at home: it is an on-paper sanity check, where you go back to first principles to uncover whether people are (or are not) going to be interested. The second pay test takes the form of a test project, where you go out there and find out for real.

Pay Test 1: does it solve a problem?

This is the basic litmus test for spotting a good free range idea.

Time: 30 minutes

Why: People are naturally interested in things that benefit them in some way – even if that is simply an emotional benefit. Why would someone else care about your product? If you don't know the answer to that then you won't know if you have a market, and you won't be able to package and present it in the right way (which sucks because you'll never make any money!). Knowing the problems you solve gives you the answers you need to move forward with confidence.

Solving a problem is your secret superpower in having people begging to buy what you have to offer. In short: if people pay for what you do, it's because it hits on something that is important to them right now – *important enough to pay to sort out.*

A problem is simply any situation your clients are unhappy about. For example: 'I can't stand this office any more. I want to do more than hang out for my next holiday but I don't know how to make that happen!' (Hello, the reason you bought this book!) So, the right question in that situation is not 'is there a market for yet another coach or consultant?' but rather 'are there people who are sinking under the weight of that problem, and who feel it so strongly that they would pay to sort it out?' In this case, the answer is a resounding *yes.*

Look for the emotions behind the reasons people might be interested: annoyed, frustrated, stuck, guilty, angry, worried, etc. Those are problem words. When you identify their problem and communicate in that person's language that you understand and can solve it, you don't need to 'convince' them, they'll already want you because they will feel your solution was created just for them. Which, in fact, it was.

Importantly the problem has to be one that your audience is aware of and feels strongly about. If it is just something that's a 'nice to have' but they are doing just fine without it, then you'll have an uphill struggle selling what you do. You shouldn't have to convince anyone they have a problem!

Finally, a problem does not have to be world-changing to be important. It just has to be important to your customers, as you will see in the exercise below:

EXERCISE   What's the problem?

Write your answers to these questions:

What is the product or service you want to use for this exercise?
Example: my quirky T-shirt company

_____

Who would you want as your target market for this offering?
Example: a certain type of middle-aged urban man

_____

What is the biggest headache, frustration or worry for people in your target niche? *(Alternatively: what would they like to be different in their lives in relation to this topic?)*

Example: this man is afraid of looking like he has turned into a boring Dad figure and desperately wants to show he still has style – but is equally worried about looking like he is stuck in his youth.

_____

Put this into melodramatic language: What is that thing that they are frustrated with, stuck on, confused by, distraught about – whatever the problem is (eg 'It's driving me crazy that...'; 'I can't take another day of...')

Example: 'It's driving me crazy that I open up the wardrobe and all my clothes look the same but when I go to the shops I don't see anything that I want except different versions of what I already have!' or 'I'm secretly afraid that I'm becoming middle-aged and boring. I feel helpless not knowing how to fix this and stupid for even worrying about it.'

What is the solution you are providing to solve that problem?

Example: my T-shirts. They are funny and clever... in an understated way. You have to look twice to get it and on the outside they are nicely stylish. He wouldn't be embarrassed if his boss saw him in one on the weekend, but he gets a boost from knowing he looks unique and his friends will ask where he got it.

Now: consider the person who would be paying for your product or service. What is the likelihood of that person handing over money for this offer based on the problems identified above? Rate this on a scale of 1–10. Go with your gut instinct here.

If you scored below an 8, your aim is to raise that score. Continue through this book and come back here as you learn more about what it takes for an idea to work, and come back and improve your description until you hit on a problem and solution mix that does work!

Now you know how you score on paper, your next test is to find out for sure by running a test project.

Pay Test 2: reality test

A short, real-world test to prove people are up for paying for this *(aka: make the damn cookies)*.

Time: Seven days

Why: A test project is the simplest and most effective way of finding out how people respond to your idea. Ian Sanders and David Sloly, authors of *Zoom: The Faster Way to Make Your Business Idea Happen* (2011), are big fans of the free range 'start small, start now' approach. They spoke to former Apple evangelist and entrepreneur Guy Kawasaki who told them:

> If you're going to go into the cookie business, Step 1 is not to plan out five years of how many chocolate chip cookies you're going to sell. Step 1 is to make a batch of cookies and see if people beyond your family will pay for it![9]

In other words, get out there and make the damn cookies.

How: 'Get it out there' does not mean 'quit your job and put all on the line for a crazy idea!' Instead, starting today, you can run a simple free range prototype project. This time your project will be a test project. This is similar to the Play Project you ran earlier in the book, but here the focus is on gaguing other people's interest in what you have to offer.

FREE RANGE ACTION   **Your first test project**

In your pay test project you get people to actually pay for something. Experimentation and real-world testing is more powerful than any focus group because it is real, and fast, and gives you outcomes you can rely on. It is one thing to say 'I'm interested' and another thing to actually put your hand in your wallet; the latter is what we get your people to do here.

◀

Your subjects don't always have to pay with actual money (although that is ideal) but if they don't they do have to give up their *time* or take *action* to prove their interest. Here are three ideas of ways to start your own test projects with what you have right now.

★ Get two paying 'test' clients for your product or service (yes, people do this in a week).

★ Run a scaled-down version of your event/course/workshop idea. Find people on Meetup.com (you can form your own group there on any topic), or by putting it up as a Facebook event and asking your friends to pass it around. Offer it for low cost in a free venue. You must charge something to check people are willing to pay, even if it is a token amount. Aim to get this going within three weeks of having the idea.

★ Hop on websites such as fiverr.com and offer your service for as low as five dollars. Yes, this is not your exact market and certainly not your real price point – but put together a good offer on a website like this and you can get your first three clients, testimonials and above all confidence as you get out there for real... without having to build a website or do any marketing. Afterwards, remove your listing and create your own brand at the price you really want.

What will you do for your test project?

_____

Once you have run your first test project, come back and consider. What worked? What didn't? Remember that your first £50 is harder to make than your first £5,000, so don't give up immediately if you get a lukewarm response. It is possible that it's because of how you are presenting it. Re-jig how you present it, using the techniques in the second half of this book, and try again. Be open to your idea evolving, too: the odds are that the idea you run with will end up being a little different to the idea in your head right now and the only way to find out which works is to get out there and run it for real.

HINT you may be wondering if you can just start without business registration. Depending on where you live and what you are doing the answer is, in many cases, yes you can. The UK, in particular, is one of the easiest places in the world to start doing business (and you do not need a registered limited company to do a £50 project!). However it's still important to learn what is and isn't needed for your individual situation; check out the 'Start For Under £100' resource pack (Chapter 13) as a starting point.

MINI CASE STUDY

I was stuck in research mode... analyzing my market, what to sell, would it work... the one thing I forgot was to actually create some art that I wanted to sell. Inspired by the free range approach, I finally picked up the brush and started painting. I created more than 60 pieces in six months.

As of last week, I've sold over 50 of my originals (plus the prints are selling really well!). I started selling at local art festivals, but now I have collectors all over the world in just one year. What I learned: staying safe doesn't get you where you want to go or any closer to your dreams. Just do something. Take action! And I did it all as a single mother with a full-time job.

Heather Dakota, Orlando, Florida, USA
www.dakotaartstudio.com

TIP   **Where are you in your idea?**

This is not just about a good idea, it's about a good idea *for you*. When you see investors on television choose an idea to back, they can select from a wide range of ideas because what they bring to the table is their years of experience of starting and growing businesses.

When you are starting your own thing, you need to bring something personally, and as a first timer usually that contribution is going to be *understanding*. Understanding means really *getting* this area or the people. It might be having an intense awareness of this topic, moving in those circles and knowing how it feels to be in your niche's shoes. It might, more practically, be having a key skill or strength that you need in order to make this happen.

Sometimes understanding comes from direct career experience. For example, when my client Susan decided to break out on her own, she drew from her experience working in luxury goods PR to set up by herself helping luxury goods brands to build their profile and reach more people. Starting in a space similar to your experience is a simple and quick way to get going as your own boss (if you're in a real hurry to get out of your job, this can be a smart move to get you started!).

However, CV-based experience is not the only type of understanding you can bring. Most free rangers bring a different type of understanding, and that is understanding based on their life experience. When Jenny (who you will meet in the branding chapter) created her project *F*ck the Diets*, she brought the understanding of having battled with diets all her life (and won), as well as her naturally supportive style. She had no professional background in this new field (her career to date had been as an IT services manager!) but that personal understanding of her niche's problem was enough to get her started.

▶

◀

What do you bring?

Jot down some thoughts on:

* ★ Why you got this idea in the first place (often a big clue is there).
* ★ What is your personal experience of this area? For example, does any of your work background give you insights into this? Have you spent money or time learning about the area? Or, more simply: have you been through the problems your people are going through?
* ★ Have you ever done any part of this in your life before? This doesn't have to be paid work, just consider whether friends come to you for help with this topic right now.
* ★ How do your personality and your natural strengths add to this idea?
* ★ What do you bring that is even 1 per cent different to other people out there doing this already? This can be a perspective or an attitude.
* ★ Imagine the day-to-day 'doing' of this idea. What excites you about this vision?

You don't need a hot answer for each of these questions, they are designed to get you thinking. One answer can be enough to show that yes, you are in this idea and this is really an idea that is good for you rather than good... for someone else.

Odds are that when you're really keen on an idea then you're going to be in there somewhere. If not, go back and consider: what could you change to make your idea more 'you'?

DOS AND DON'TS

Dos and don'ts of figuring out if your idea will work

DON'T use Dragons' Den and the hottest sexiest new launches as your benchmark for what works. Those examples are profiled because they are unusual, not because they are the norm.

DO realize that a great idea doesn't always sound great on paper (and an idea that's great on paper isn't always great in practice).

DO remember that people don't pay for a skill or a personality trait, they pay for results. Instead of asking 'how can I get paid for this trait' ask 'how can this trait be of value to someone else?'

DO ask yourself: 'does this solve a problem that is bothering someone enough that they would pay to sort it out?'

DON'T assume that what someone else charges for this is your personal charging limit.

DO the £50 test. Make it a rule that, if you like an idea, you stick with it until you earn your first £50. Then you can revise it. This takes the pressure off thinking it has to be a 'forever' commitment and lets you find out a lot about the idea as you reach that goal. Also, you get £50.

DO think smart. If you already know people are making a living from your idea then there is no need to reinvent that wheel: their existence proves customers are paying (just make sure they really are making a living not just doing it as a hobby). Instead focus on discovering where you are in this idea, and making sure it is solving a problem people care about. Think like a free ranger and adapt these exercises to your situation: there's always a gap in the market for people who think smart.

FREE RANGE PROFILE SUSAN'S STORY – FROM IDEA TO INCOME IN 10 WEEKS

Susan Moolman had a high-flying career doing in-house PR for an interior designer, yet while she enjoyed the glitz and the glam of that world, she knew she wanted something more. Frankly, she was sick of the packed commutes and spending her summers trapped in the office:

> *I remember* those *days in the office... the ones when I would rather stick a fork in my eye than churn out another report or have to think up another excuse for why I'm 10 minutes late on a day where I had nothing pressing to do anyway.*

Then, Susan moved from New York to London, and took this opportunity to change her work-life as well as her location. Susan knew the lifestyle she wanted. She no longer wanted to work for someone else: she wanted to be in charge of where, when and how she worked.

But there was a snag: Susan had no idea what she wanted to *do*. All she knew was that whatever she chose had to generate an income that would allow her to purchase that Burberry jacket she'd fallen in love with the week I met her for coffee in Soho: 'I still have to be able to buy beautiful things!' she said, 'that's not something I can give up'. (This might be the first jacket-inspired life change.)

To figure things out, Susan signed up to my coaching programme, and after the first week I was hit by the realization that I'd just met someone who is a wonderful bundle of energy who *makes things happen*.

In less than ten weeks Susan had:

1 figured out what she wanted to do;

2 launched her new business;

3 landed her first major client... the designer Nicky Haslam (the girl aims high!).

To get started fast in her new free range life, all Susan needed was a website, which she created herself in Wordpress. She got a friend to design a logo, wrote the copy herself and asked clients for images of their work. From there things grew fast: Susan emailed me to share that she had billed her clients about £40,000 in the first six months and since then her business has gone from strength to strength.

Q&A WITH FREE RANGE SUSAN

What was the moment you figured out what you wanted to do?

'The best thing I did was the exercise where you match up things you love with what you have to offer – that was the 'lightbulb' moment for me! Once I figured that out it was pretty easy for things to fall into place.'

Did you end up buying that Burberry jacket?

'Yes! There was also the day where I bought myself *three* Jimmy Choo handbags. The oily green one with the snakeskin handles paid for the entire experience when Nicky noticed it straight away on our first meeting and said, 'What a great bag'. A girl's gotta do what a girl's gotta do!'

What is your advice for people reading this book?

'Don't downplay the scariness of it. It is shit scary. Particularly if you're going it alone. But if you believe that there is a market for your product or service, the only way you'll know whether it will work or not is to just go for it. If you don't, that nagging little voice in the back of your head will forever be telling you, 'What if...'

The best advice I have to give is: 'Fake it till you make it.' If everyone else believes that you can do something, it's only a matter of willpower and time until you do it.'

Susan isn't a magician. She didn't stumble across opportunities by luck. She was just smart, self-aware and determined to put in the time and energy to make a real change.

EXERCISE   **Part 3 reflections – your starting point**

Now it's time to pull together your thoughts from this section.

This is the space to capture the idea that you are most keen to move forward with. So: what free range career idea is most attractive to you right now?

I want to start my free range career by offering (give a summary of your idea):

_____

This will give me the freedom to:

_____

(for example, get paid to do what I love/have, more time/work, where I choose, etc)

On the scale of 1–10 of how much this possibility will rock my life I give it a:

_____

NOTE   If you are just reading this book without doing the actions (ahem) you might still be uncertain which free range career you want to take forward. That's fine. For the purposes of helping you work through Part 4, simply write down whichever seems most attractive right now. You can always come back and change your answer as you discover more about it!

What tip could you use from the Original Idea chapter (Chapter 9) to make your free range offering more unique?

_____

▶

What did you find in your Advantage Case? (Chapter 10)

_____

Which free range business types (eg: services, virtual products, physical products, advertising, or a blend) were most attractive to you? (Chapter 11)

_____

What were your favourite resources in the 'Start For Under £100' pack? (Chapter 12)

_____

What did you learn from pay test 1: the problem-solving exercise? (Chapter 13)

_____

What you are going to do for pay test 2: your first test project? (Chapter 13)

_____

CONGRATULATIONS! You reached the end of Part 3. Now we move to the next step, looking at how free rangers go from an idea to full-time income (in a way that lets their personality shine and their lifestyle dreams become reality).

Notes

1   http://www.mediabistro.com/prnewser/vocus-acquires-help-a-reporter-out-haro_b3853

2   Gartner, John D (2005) *The Hypomanic Edge: The link between (a little) craziness and (a lot of) success in America*, Simon & Schuster, New York

3   Boynton, A and Fischer, B (2011) *The Idea Hunter: How to find the best ideas and make them happen*, Jossey-Bass, New York

4   Daisy is in her early twenties and is by far the youngest person profiled in this book. I have included her for younger readers, to show that you don't need a job to break away from in order to go free range. For older readers, don't use age as a reason why not! Daisy's original work was on weekends and evenings and could have been started around a regular job! See her videos at www.daisyjenks.co.uk

5   See Emma and her crew changing the way the 'world works' at www.e3reloaded.com

6   http://www.ted.com/speakers/dan_cobley.html

7   Adams, Scott, How to Get a Real Education, *The Wall Street Journal* [Online] http://online.wsj.com/article/SB10001424052748704101604 576247143383496656.html

8   After years of adventures in the ChocStar van http://www.chocstar.co.uk as of this year Petra is exploring a different free range project: http://www.eat.st that aims to transform the British foodscape through fabulous street food.

9   Sanders, I and Sloly, D (2011) *Zoom: The Faster Way to Make Your Business Idea Happen*, Financial Times/Prentice Hall, London

INTERLUDE
FREE RANGE
REALITY
CHECK

As you start on this journey you are bound to hear people tell you to 'be realistic' about your options. Those voices can be quite off-putting, so I wanted to show you another perspective before we move on to how to make your new life happen. The next three chapters have no exercises and no actions... just a rush of reasons why yes, this is possible, and why a negative voice is not necessarily a reason to give up. Grab a cup of tea, sit back and enjoy a free range reality check.

15 MEET THE PEOPLE WHO DON'T WANT YOU TO ESCAPE THE CAREER CAGE

(or: the beige army unmasked)

'Keep away from people who try to belittle your
ambitions. Small people always do that, but the really
great make you feel that you, too, can become great.'

Mark Twain

This chapter's message is really important but it's one that some
people (some people who you and I both know) won't want
you to read.

These people, the ones we both know, are a type that you come
across every day (shh, there's one in the office with you now!). They
prefer tradition and routine to innovation and enthusiasm, and
think that your dream of a freer, more fulfilled life is a dangerous
fantasy best quashed soon.

They are the beige army, and they have more of an impact on
your life than you realize.

The beige army are the managers in the office who can't see the
big picture – they prefer to nit-pick on the 1 per cent negative instead: 'Yes, well done for launching that project that might change
the world, but you didn't fill in this line in form 30B in triplicate.'

The beige army are staid, repressed and terrified of change, but
that's not why I have a problem with them. After all, it's up to them
how they live their lives. I have a problem because they want *you* to
be that way too.

They wander around the corridors of your office block (and,
perhaps, your extended family reunions) judging anyone who does
anything outside of *their* comfort zone.

Should you be so audacious as to consider an option (for yourself) that the beige army finds challenging to *their* beliefs, they purse their lips and say: 'Are you sure that's wise?' They furrow their brows and ask: 'Why would you want to do that? Why don't you just get another job?'

Ever heard that? Then you know that it's not a question, it's a statement: what they really mean is:

If you do that strange thing you will crash and burn and fail and you will be laughed at. No one will be on your side and you will end up in the gutter, miserable, hearkening back to the golden days when you were safe here, safe with us in this beige existence where nothing changes, ever.

That's what the beige army wants you to think whenever you consider making a change outside of *their* comfort zone. Venture to voice a different perspective and, certain of their world view, they'll curl their lips with a little smug sneer and say 'yes, alright darling'. And almost certainly ignore you.

The truth is the beige army is just a group of scared but vocal people

All of us get scared about our lives:

★ Are we the person we imagined we'd be?

★ What if this is all there is to life after all?

★ What if we get it wrong? What if we get it right?

★ What if it turns out we are not good enough after all?

These are big scary questions.

If you've asked yourself any of those questions – felt the fear, and admitted to yourself that you were scared – then you are not a member of the beige army. All of us get scared, that is part of being human: what's really evil is that the beige army won't own up to their fear.

The man in the beige army doesn't look like a terrified animal but he is. His criticisms of others are his weapon against facing up to his feelings. He is living a lie: he pretends he is doing the 'right' thing; he pretends this so much that he no longer remembers he is pretending. All he knows is that if one of those 'other' people who are 'different' from him come on his turf, he gets het up. Any alternative is far too scary for him to contemplate.

Everything the beige army says is a manifestation of their fear. For example:

1 **They question your worthiness:** The beige army hears about your idea for a blog and says, 'how can you write on that when you don't have a PhD in the topic?' or 'are you sure it's wise to start without a reputation?'

   They don't dare to do anything without 'qualifications' and permission, because they have never believed in themselves (so why should you?).

2 **They criticize from the outside without putting themselves on the line:** the beige army are the (anonymous) online critics who harshly rip into 20 books on starting a business, but never get the guts to start a business themselves; the people who look at your project and criticize details without daring to start their own thing.

   They don't dare, because they think that people will be as harsh and critical of them as they are of other people.

3 **They make you feel small and naïve:** the beige army are the people who hear your plan, put on thin smiles and say, 'meanwhile back on planet earth'. Or they'll snort and say, 'good luck with that'.

   They make you feel small, because believing that any other possibility exists calls into question their life choices; they can't stand feeling vulnerable.

Ever heard from someone like that and questioned yourself as a result? You are not alone. I have seen people on the edge of making changes give up because of someone else's fears.

Yet thinking and acting in this way has got the beige person to where they are now. So ask yourself: do you want to be in their shoes? Do you want their job, their holidays, their attitude and their life? If so, take their advice, because that's the way to get there.

The beige army's biggest weapon is its pretence that it represents everyone

In their worldview, everyone has a job:

> *Do you want to throw away your career and be a weird broke hippie? Everyone knows that it's a bad, hard world out there: the most sensible thing to do is stay safe, keep your head down.*

Everyone knows that.

Of course, everyone doesn't think like this. But as the beige army is so vocal and certain, you'd be forgiven for thinking otherwise. It's hard to do something against what 'most people do': most of us don't want to be 'odd' or 'not quite normal', do we? That human desire for acceptance and inclusion is what the beige army banks on to keep you in line.

But the beige army *are not the normal ones*. They are the sad repressed folk who live their lives barely feeling anything any more. They've turned off their emotions inside and they want you to do that too. They are not the majority, they are just loud.

So let's call them out for what they are. The people who say 'it's not possible', 'that's a bit weird' or 'why don't you just get a job' do not speak for society and they do not speak for you. They are just a group: the beige army, and they're dead scared of getting any bright, lively paints on their bland beige uniform.

How to overcome the beige army (your battle plan)

Once you've named them for what they are (the 'beige army', not 'everyone'), there are three things you can do to stop them from stopping *you* moving forward:

1. Know you are not one of them

The beige army is a big group: mostly because they are so good at influencing others by making you feel small if you act differently. It's easy to be taken in by their certainty, and even adopt their characteristics.

Here's the difference – if you act like a beige soldier you'll hate yourself a little for it ('oh my god, I've become a bureaucrat!') whereas they pride themselves on being mundane. Whenever you recognize that in yourself, a moment of difference in attitude, hold on to it, because daring to be different is your shield from their attacks.

2. Be human

Be enthusiastic and surround yourself with folk who are free range thinkers. Displays of passion – be it talking enthusiastically or showing emotion – are terrifying to the beige army. They will laugh at it and belittle it: 'alright, tone it down there', 'hmm, getting a bit carried away?'

However, Brené Brown, a research professor who has spent the past 10 years researching vulnerability, courage and shame with thousands of people, points out:

You cannot selectively numb emotion. You can't say, 'here's vulnerability, here's shame, here's disappointment: I don't want to feel them so here's a beer and a banana nut muffin.' You can't numb those hard feelings without numbing the other emotions. When we numb hard feelings, we numb joy, we numb gratitude, we numb happiness. And then we are miserable and we are looking for purpose and meaning. [1]

So don't listen to the beige army call to keep mum and keep numb. Instead, find your true tribe and spend time with them: immerse yourself in their writing, their events, their experiences; share their passion and soon you'll stop seeing the beige army as the 'normal' ones but as strange creatures to be pitied.

3. Use your secret weapon

Here's the biggest thing you can do to fight them: don't. The beige army are impenetrable people who – in the name of avoiding discomfort – have numbed themselves from feeling.

A beige person is like a rock: nothing moves them so don't bother trying. There is no point trying to convert them. Just walk around them. (Then, when you end up doing well, they'll change tack and pretend they were on your side all the way.)

I'm taking on the beige army, but I'm not interested in beating them. This isn't about winning an ideological argument with a group of terrified people. It's about getting around the big, critical, scared blob of a barrier in your way so that you can live your own life.

Once you're on the other side you'll look back and wonder why they ever had any power over you. You'll smile, turn your back on their fear, and walk forward into your real life in full colour.

16 WHAT TO DO WITH THOSE REASONS WHY NOT

'Argue for your limitations and, sure enough,
they're yours.' *Richard Bach*

The 'not for the likes of me' myth

*'Sure, these stories are nice but there are a lot of reasons why I can't
do this.*

*They had an advantage that I don't have – it's nice to dream but
my situation is different; I have so many Reasons Why Not.'*

Myth buster

In writing this book, I have spoken to some of my favourite free
rangers who broke out of their careers to go and create lives most
people dream of. At the same time, I've also been speaking more and
more to the people who desperately want to do the same, but feel stuck.

The single thing that separates the ones who broke out from the
ones who haven't is stupidly simple. It's not money. It's not age. It's
not some smart strategy they are yet to hear.

It's their attitude to the Reasons Why Not.

I actually want to slap myself down for saying that. How clichéd
is that? Have the right attitude and you'll succeed? What a load of
rubbish. Except for the part where it's true. *Darn that reality.*

I have spoken with Free Range Humans of all backgrounds: people
with kids, or without. Graduates from the top schools in the world, and
university dropouts. CVs spanning every industry you can imagine.

On paper, these people are wildly different from one another.
But when it came to handling the Reasons Why Not you could
map their words over each other:

Melissa Morgan: 'Not knowing enough is not a reason why you can't do this. I knew nothing about business when I started. I learnt everything by myself. In today's world no one can honestly say they can't find information.'

Benny Lewis: 'Any excuse you can come up with someone has gotten around it. You could have no natural talent, it doesn't matter, a lot of idiots do great things. You could be as poor as you can imagine – people do it. I tell people to look at people like Helen Keller who was a blind and deaf woman in the 19th century yet wrote books, spoke multiple languages, met two American presidents – imagine what she had to overcome, and tell me how you can come up with excuses why you can't do something?'

Peter Shankman: 'There's always going to be a reason why you can't do this. We all have bills to pay. Find ways around the barriers.'

Why is this so important? Because the inverse is debilitating. Corbett Barr, blogger and online entrepreneur, explains:

There are people who look for unfair advantages *when they hear about someone's success story. They like to point out connections, money, special talents and other reasons why success was possible [and] why they couldn't do the same thing.*

Looking for 'gotcha' advantages in other people's stories misses the point. Naysayers ignore the perseverance and incredible effort the hero in question had to bring to the table. They ignore the obstacles overcome on the journey.

Whether you habitually attempt to discredit others' successes might tell you something about your own chances of success.[2]

Why should someone else's advantages be your limitations?

Free range third way

Instead of focusing on what you don't have, do what every Free Range Human does and focus on maximizing what you do have (if you struggle here, go back to the Advantage Case exercise in Chapter 10).

Also, get into the habit of picking your similarities to – rather than differences from – the people in success stories. For example, pick a success story that you find attractive. What similarities do you have to that person? No 'buts', just list the similarities.

Now, imagine that same person before they made a change. What excuses could they have used that the change was not possible? Remember: they didn't know it would work when they started, so what reasons could they have found to prove that they were at a disadvantage?

Then, get aware that when you *do* do that Impossible Thing That You Just Can't Do Right Now, people will pick at least one item off your advantage list above, and they will say: 'Oh, *of course* they made it happen, they had *that* thing so it was all easy for them.'

After you pick your jaw off the floor, you'll know that wasn't true. You'll know you still overcame obstacles and worked hard for it. Exactly like every other person who has done something out of the norm.

No matter how many how-tos we learn, there will always be a Reason Why Not. How you handle your Reasons Why Not is the greatest indicator of where you will be this time next year.

DOS AND DON'TS

Dos and don'ts of starting (at your age)

DONT believe that inner voice that tells you you're 'too old' or 'trapped by a mortgage'. I was 43 when I realized I didn't want to continue working 12 hours a day to pay for the mortgage on a house I rarely saw. I sold the house and resigned from my well-paid job. Now I live in the centre of beautiful Seville, coaching, writing and teaching for a living – and I love it! A far cry from my old careers as special adviser to a government minister and communications director for a multinational.

Alison Broom, Seville, Spain, **www.sevillanlife.com**

I'm a young woman running a company in a very hierarchical part of the world. Sometimes people are surprised when they come to meet the CEO and it's me! I've been told more than once that I shouldn't be doing this. But don't let that stop you – the quality of your work will speak for itself. You just can't let other people's opinions of your age hold you back.

Emma Reynolds, Hong Kong, **www.e3reloaded.com**

DO realize that people at every age think they are either too young or too old. There is no perfect age, only now.

DO realize you can use your age to your advantage. For example, if you are older than average you will come across as more experienced even if you are new to a field, so use that. If you are younger, people tend to assume you have a fresh and sharp perspective – feel free to play on that.

DON'T expect other people to accept you until you accept yourself. The biggest barrier with age is when you are uncomfortable with it yourself and haven't put in place strategies to make it work for you. Get yourself comfortable with your age, and other people's perceptions will follow.

DO remember the words of Julia Cameron in *The Artist's Way*: 'Do you know how old you will be by the time you learn to play the piano? The same age you will be if you don't.'

MINI CASE STUDY

In my forties I decided I wanted a change from the nine to five office drudge. So one morning on my way to work I saw a guy working in our local park and thought, that looks good, I'll do that.

Long story short – it took me eight months of hassling the local council to hire me and eventually they gave me a job (hoping it would kill me, I think). I was located with a hot-mix (bitumen) gang and my job was to dig up the patches of road that needed repairing, then throw it on the back of the truck, and then shovel the hot mix into it. Very hard work physically. I was only 8 stone. At the end of the day I could just make it home, eat and go to bed. Women didn't do that kind of work in those days so I was also a bit of a trailblazer.

But I *loved* it, and got so fit, and after a year or so I decided to be a fitness instructor, so I got qualified and worked my own hours in gyms, which then led me to being interested in people and how they operate, which led me to life coaching, which is what I do now.

I am now in my sixties, which I know sounds ancient but believe me that is just a crock. Another excuse to give up. I am an avid cyclist and runner and have a fantastic relationship of 25 years. We travel and work around Australia, doing what we love and having fun. I recently acquired my NLP Practitioner qualification and just love learning, and want other people to realize they can pretty much do anything, regardless of age.

Joan Bell, Australia[3]

FREE RANGE PROFILE JON'S STORY – 'HOW TO QUIT YOUR JOB, MOVE TO PARADISE AND GET PAID TO CHANGE THE WORLD'

This is a guest chapter by Jon Morrow, full-time blogger and Free Range Human. He has a story I think you need to hear. Whatever you had planned for the next 10 minutes put it down and read this. Really.

Jon's story

It's fun to dream about your blog or business idea taking off and changing your life, but sometimes you wonder if it's just that: a dream. This is the real world, and in the real world, dreams don't really come true.

Right?

Well, let me tell you a little story...

This is how I quit my job

In April 2006, I was hit by a car going 85 miles an hour.

I didn't see him coming, and I don't remember much about the accident, but I do remember being pulled out of my minivan with my shirt on fire. The front end of the van was torn off, gasoline was everywhere, and my legs were broken in 14 places.

For the next three months, I had nothing to do but endure the pain and think about my life. I thought about my childhood. I thought about my dreams. I thought about my career.

And overall, I decided I didn't like the way things were going.

So I quit.

Hearing about my insanity, a friend called and asked me, 'Well, what are you going to do now?'

'I don't know,' I told him. 'Maybe start a blog.'

And so that's what I did.

For the next three months, I didn't just tinker around with blogging, I dedicated myself to it. I started work at 8 in the morning and I kept going until 11 at night. I didn't watch television. I didn't see my friends. From morning till night, I was writing, reading and connecting with other bloggers. Nothing else.

Within two months it was getting 2,000 visitors a day and was nominated for best business/money blog of the year. A couple of months after that Brian Clark asked me to become the Associate Editor of Copyblogger, and so I sold for five figures and went to work at one of the most popular blogs in the world.

And, amazingly, that's just the beginning of the story.

How I moved to paradise

Have you ever woken up one day and realized you secretly despise everything about where you live? The weather is horrible. Your neighbours are jerks. You don't like inviting anyone to your home, because it's always a wreck, and you're ashamed of how it looks.

Well, that's exactly what happened to me in January 2009. I was sitting in my pathetic apartment, wrapped up in blankets to keep warm, trying to get some work done on the computer, when it struck me how monumentally stupid it was.

I was a full-time blogger, for God's sakes. I could do my work from anywhere in the world. Why on Earth was I living in this hellhole?

The only problem was I had no idea where I wanted to go, but a couple of weeks later, the telephone rang, and it was a friend who had retired to Mazatlan, Mexico. As usual, he was calling to gloat about the weather and the food, but instead of just suffering through it this time, I stopped him and said, 'No, don't tell me any more. I'm moving there.'

'What? When?' he stammered.

'I don't know exactly when,' I told him, 'but I'm starting right now.'

Two months later, I took a one-week trip to scout it out and look for places to live. When I got back, I started selling all of my stuff, packing the rest of it into storage, and saying goodbye to friends.

Almost one year to the day after our phone call, I hopped in the car and drove just shy of 3,000 miles to my new beachfront condo in the finest resort in Mazatlan.

As I write this, I'm sitting on my balcony with my laptop, watching (no kidding) dolphins jumping out in the Pacific. It's a sunny day, there's a nice breeze, and I'm thinking about ordering a piña colada from the restaurant downstairs.

Lucky me, right?

Well, what might surprise you is I left out a piece of the story. It's the part where I have a fatal disease. I can't move from the neck down, and yet I essentially get paid to help people.

Let's talk about that part next.

How I get paid to change the world

You know what's funny?

The worst part about having SMA [spinal muscular atrophy] isn't how everyone treats you like a charity case. It's not the frustration, anger or depression. It's not even the inability to reach over and pinch a cute girl's butt when you want to (although that's pretty bad).

No, the worst part is the freakin' *bills*. The doctors. The medication. The nurses.

I added it all up, and the total cost of keeping me alive in the US was $127,000 a year. That's not rent. That's not food. That's *just* medical expenses.

Granted, I didn't actually have to pay all that. I had private insurance, Medicaid, other government aid programs, but all that support comes at a price: they control you. The government allotted me only $700 a month to live on, and I had to spend every single cent above that on medical expenses, or they would cut me off.

So for years, that's what I did. If I made $5,000 one month, I set aside $700 for living expenses, and I spent the other $4,300 on medical bills. Nothing was left. Ever.

And eventually, I got sick of it.

I wanted to make money without having to worry about losing my healthcare. I wanted to take care of my family, instead of them always having to take care of me. I wanted to actually live somewhere *nice*, not some ratty little apartment built for folks below the poverty line.

The only problem was it just wasn't possible for me in the US.

No matter how I played with the numbers, I couldn't make it work. So, I did something crazy: I quit Medicaid. I moved to Mexico. I stopped worrying about myself at all and started a business based on one simple idea: helping people.

I found up-and-coming writers who wanted a mentor, and I trained them. I found businesses who wanted to cash in on social media, and I developed their strategy.

In exchange, they paid me what they could. Some folks gave me $50 an hour and others $300 an hour, but I treated them all the same, and I dedicated myself to making *their* dreams a reality.

The results?

Within two months, I was making so much money so fast PayPal shut down my account under suspicions of fraudulent activity. Today, not only am I making more than enough to take care of myself, but a couple of months ago, I got uppity and bought my father a car.

Do you understand how precious that is? For a guy who can't move from the neck down to buy his father a car?

And the best part is, I'm not making money doing mindless drudgery. I'm *changing people's lives*.

Every day, I get emails from readers who say my posts have changed their thinking. Every day, I get emails from students who say my advice has changed their writing. Every day, I get emails from clients who say my strategies have changed the way they do business.

I can't really believe it. Normally, a guy like me would be wasting away in a nursing home somewhere, watching television and waiting to die, but here I am speaking into a microphone and essentially getting paid to change the world. If my fingers worked, I'd pinch myself.

And here's the thing: I don't want it for just me. I want it for you too.

The reason I told you this whole story wasn't just to brag but also to convince you of one incontrovertible point:

You can do this!

You want to quit your job and become a professional blogger? You can.

You want to travel around the world, living life to its fullest?
You can.

You want to dedicate your every hour to helping people and making the world a better place?
You can.

Because listen... I know it's horribly cliché, but if I can quit my job, risk the government carting me off to a nursing home because I can't afford my own healthcare, convince my poor mother to abandon her career and drive my crippled butt 3,000 miles to a foreign country, and then make enough money to support myself, my mother, my father, and an entire nursing staff using nothing but my voice then what can you accomplish if you really set your mind to it?

My guess: pretty much anything.

No, it won't be easy. At some point, I *guarantee* you'll want to quit. I *guarantee* people will treat you like you're insane. I *guarantee* you'll cry yourself to sleep, wondering if you made a horrible mistake.

But never stop believing in yourself. The world is full of naysayers, all of them eager to shout you down at the slightest indication you might transcend mediocrity, but the greatest sin you can commit is to allow yourself to become one of them. Our job isn't to join that group, but to silence it, to accomplish things so great and unimaginable that its members are too awed to speak.

You can do it.

I believe in you.

So get started.

Right freaking now.

This article originally appeared in longer form on
www.problogger.com.[4]
Many thanks to Darren Rowse of Problogger and Jon Morrow for permission to share it here. Jon's current free range project is
www.boostblogtraffic.com

Notes

1 Brené Brown: The power of vulnerability [Video file].
   http://www.ted.com/talks/brene_brown_on_vulnerability.html
2 Corbett Barr, 'Do You Turn Advantages Into Limitations?' 15 March
   2012. http://www.corbettbarr.com/advantages-into-limitations
3 Joan's current project is www.lifecoach101.com
4 How To Quit Your Job, Move To Paradise, And Get Paid To Change
   The World. http://www.problogger.net/archives/2011/05/18/how-to-
   quit-your-job-move-to-paradise-and-get-paid-to-change-the-world

PART 4
BUILD YOUR FREE RANGE ESCAPE HATCH

17 MAKING A LIVING WITHOUT AN OFFICE
(or a boss)

'Crazy ambition requires radical practicality.

Otherwise, it's just... crazy.' *Danielle La Porte*

So far you have been through a crash course in thinking like a free ranger: you have learnt how to figure out what you want, busted the myths and discovered what you need (and what you don't): now it's time to look at what it takes to launch out of there for real.

When I first decided to launch my own thing, I walked into a bookshop and bought a book about business building (yes, they had actual bookshops back then). I can't remember the book's name because I never finished reading it.

It was red, in a nice friendly workbook size, all about the steps you need to take in order to launch your venture in 20 weeks. Or something. All I remember is that I stopped reading it because it was overwhelming. And scary. Oh, and boring.

Man was that book boring.

First, I never thought I wanted a *business*. I wanted to make a living on my own terms, without an office or a boss – ever again – and yes that meant being self-employed. But I hadn't gone into this because I loved the idea of being a (deep voice) 'business owner'. I wanted a nice life, you know? One where I could sleep in and not have to ask for permission to go on holiday, and where I got to do lots of things I loved. Somehow, that book (and the others on the shelves around it) forgot about us. Nothing in there was about the entire reason I wanted to make this change; what about the *life* that was meant to come after the job?

The book made it feel like business launching was another world. One that I'd rather put to one side and get to later. *Someday*.

It wasn't until I got started that I realized something profound: conventional step-by-step books on starting a small business aren't about building a business. Most business-building products tell you how to create a business *shell*.

I would read things like: Step 1, Choose a name; Step 2, Register and fill in the paperwork; Step 3, Create a logo.

Fine. You can follow these steps, and you'll get something that looks like a nice professional business. Pity about the part where it's not bringing in money. The part where you learn how to do things in a smarter way than most struggling freelancers? Oh you can learn that later, the logic goes. No wonder people think that making money by yourself is a bit of a mystery.

So there I was, sitting with a pile of books that made me want to go to sleep (or panic) and a bunch of things that I thought I *should* be doing and a heap of 'argh' whenever I tried to work out which one to start with. And still no clue as to how any of it would bring in consistent good money.

What I know now

Back then, my vision of business was what I now call 'old style business'. The difference between old and new style businesses is something you're going to find out about in the rest of this book.

If you're all up for the freedom of making a living by yourself, but feeling a bit *ugh* about this whole business-building malarkey, I guarantee you're thinking of old style business. However, it is the new style 'break the rules and make it yours' free range way of working that we're going to explore here.

But how will I pay the bills?

This question gives me the chills.

Imagine you're about to get on a plane with a trainee pilot. You already know the touchdown might be a tad bumpier than normal, sure, that's to be expected. However, the one question you don't want to hear him ask is *how can I make the plane stay in the air?*

That is the same as a free range fledgling asking about paying the bills. These are very good questions, yes, but both have an undertone of believing that is the very best you can expect. They suggest that paying the bills and somehow just staying afloat is all you can hope for.

If that's *all* you want, read a formulaic start-up guide, or go to a night class in a local college. There are a lot of ways to launch something average. But that's not what we are about. *You deserve more than average.*

Free ranging is about creating your ultimate life. Reaching your potential, building on that moment of magic you have to offer and creating a darn good income to boot. Freedom and fulfilment *and* a great income. No compromises.

Let's get real here

This stuff you're going to read about here works. But it doesn't work if you just go through the motions. Standing out, getting status, turning an idea into income, is not a clever trick. I know it may sound fluffy, but the truth is you can't fake this. You cannot beige this up. Every time someone tries to pretend, and makes an inauthentic business decision to make a quick buck, that will be the decision that backfires.

You're going into this for a reason – for the life you want and to feel good about what you do, every day. I can give you the techniques to help this happen but there's a big part you have to play. This is about bringing the whole of you to the party.

After all, at the end of the day, you're not building a business, you're creating a life. You in?

18 WHY YOU DON'T NEED A BUSINESS PLAN
(or an MBA)

'Nothing will ever be attempted if all possible objections must first be overcome.' *Samuel Johnson*

The first step to working for yourself is often assumed to be 'hole up alone in a room and write a long business plan'. Here's why you should be doing the exact opposite.

The 'research' myth

'Before I start properly I need to spend months researching, and write a detailed business plan.'

Myth buster

Get this: at your stage, most planning is really guessing.

> *Unless you're a fortune teller, long-term business planning is a fantasy. There are just too many factors that are out of your hands... Why don't we just call plans what they really are: guesses. Start referring to your business plans as business guesses, your financial plans as financial guesses, and your strategic plans as strategic guesses...*
>
> *The timing of long-range plans is screwed up too. You have the most information when you're doing something, not before you've done it. Yet when do you write a plan? Usually before you've even begun. That's the worst time to make a decision.*
>
> Jason Fried and David Heinemeier Hansson, founders of 37signals and authors of *ReWork*.[1]

This applies double to free range businesses. You see, the main purpose of a business plan is to help you raise funding by convincing someone else that your idea has potential. But as a Free Range Human you're not looking for funding – you're starting small, so the only thing that matters is real world results.

In other words: you don't need a long business plan. Yes, you definitely should have a good idea where you're going. *But you can do that on the back of a beer mat.*

In fact, spending months tinkering with a traditional business plan might actively hold you back. I once heard an interview with a guy called Andrew, whose first venture failed. When asked why he said:

> *The biggest mistake we made was being completely encumbered by this vision of what I wanted it to be and taking 10 months to build the product, all the while making assumptions on what people want... You're way too dumb to figure out if your idea is good. It's up to the masses. So build that very small thing and get it out there.*[2]

That guy was Andrew Mason, founder of Groupon – one of the biggest business successes of the decade. The above was the reason why his first venture didn't work out... and why Groupon did.

What does this mean in practice? Well, if you want to educate people, don't sit around figuring out how many folders you might need next July. Instead, one evening after work, run a micro prototype project with 10 people. Find your very first guinea pigs wherever you can – maybe go to Meetup.com and start a new group or ask your friends if they know anyone. Once you've done this you're not some person who will 'one day' start an education business. *You're actually in business.*

I'd been 'just thinking about' going free range for years and had been flitting from one idea to the other (always at the 'research' rather than the 'doing' stage). I'd typically say, 'I'm not ready yet', overcomplicate things to the point of 'paralysis through analysis', and overwhelm myself. The free range approach has taught me how to simplify things, not to wait until everything is perfect, and take manageable steps in the right direction. When I actually put myself out there I gained a client out of the blue through Twitter, showing me that this really is possible, and the steps I'm taking are being rewarded.

Mark Scanlon, Suffolk, UK

Free range third way

Someone who takes this philosophy to heart is my friend Terri Belford. Some years back, Terri fell in love with a small seaside town. She wanted to get back into art, and this place seemed like the perfect location for a gallery. She found a venue in October... and made a commitment to open the gallery on Thanksgiving weekend at the end of November. Terri explains:

My only experience with the art business was selling my work at craft fairs when I was very young, so I spent the next few weeks going to open studios, chatting with artists and trying to figure out what sells. I gave myself a virtual MBA in the local art scene in a few weeks!

Because I don't believe in putting a lot of money into start-ups, I talked about 50 artists and craftspeople into working on a consignment basis – they lent me their art and they got paid when it sold. My son and I then headed to the lumberyard for plywood to build display pedestals. A few weeks later, we were in business.

Because Terri started free range style, she was able to adapt as she learned more on the ground. For example:

Some of the merchandise I started with turned out to be wrong for the clientele. But I didn't lose money. I simply returned it to the artists, grateful I hadn't invested upfront, and picked up more of the pieces that were selling well. Things took off from there.

Within the first couple of years, the business had outgrown its location, and I was earning a good income. When it was time to move on, I sold the business for a very nice six figures.[3]

Terri didn't waste time worrying *I've never sold art professionally* or *I need to spend 12 months researching and creating a 100-page business plan.* She didn't do what other people might do: sink money into an expensive space, then try to raise funds to buy some art and then hope it sells. Actually most people would not do that: they would *think* they had to take that risky approach and then give up before starting.

Instead, Terri started small, learnt fast, then flexed and adapted to what worked (and what didn't). You can do that too: even if it is in a side-project while still in your job.

You see, it isn't about closing your eyes and jumping in blind. Free range successes evolve as an iterative process of learning and doing. *Learn an idea*, try it out, *learn a technique*, test again, *learn what works*, get out there... *oh look, you've launched and it's working!* That's a much smarter approach than spending months on a plan before you know what really works.

While it's up to you to do the 'doing', the rest of this book is going to help you with the 'learning'. I'm going to share the strategies that will give you the edge in getting your free range journey off the ground and thriving. To get the most out of this, as you read, keep your mind ticking over to find ways of trying out these concepts by taking your own free range action, ASAP.

TIP   Beating the 'perfectionism freeze'

If you have a perfectionist streak (welcome to the club!) the concept of starting small and starting fast might be somewhat jarring.

Your Top Dog (the yappy inner critic you met earlier) would much prefer it if you holed up for 12 months writing a plan. He is likely to bark out messages about failure, and tell you that you *must* be certain that you will excel at every single step you take (even if that step is from the safety of your own computer). Top Dog's fear of failure is contagious. Here's how to deal with that.

When you start thinking 'what if I waste time on this project and it doesn't work out?' Or 'what if I start and I don't like it?' ask yourself another question: 'What is the cost of *not* starting?'

It is all too easy to forget that there is a cost to staying where you are now. That cost is your life, and specifically, your finite time.

When someone asks 'what if something goes wrong?', my reply is: something is going wrong right now. Look at how long you have been dreaming about this. Consider how you feel. Consider that you are giving up your best cognitive hours of your life to something that doesn't feel right at all. *Consider that you already knew this all that time ago yet nothing has changed.*

Now ask yourself again: 'what has been the cost of *not* starting to date?' You may not know for sure whether it would have been a waste of time to start something but you do know the cost of not starting due to 'what ifs'. The only thing that will definitely not work out is doing nothing.

So don't get hung up on making a mistake. You're starting in a safe space – not putting your income on the line with each experiment! From now on, mistakes are just another way of learning what works and what doesn't. Remember there is no prize for getting each step perfect first time around, and no penalty for having a prototpe project mess-up.

It's fine to try something out before you're ready. In fact it's not just fine, it's essential. That's how every successful free ranger made their new life happen. Now it's your turn. As you read the rest of this book, get ready to take action, and explore this new world on your terms.

19 WHY YOU DON'T NEED TO APPEAL TO EVERYONE

'When you innovate, you've got to be prepared
for people telling you that you are nuts.'

Larry Ellison, Founder, Oracle

Here is where it all begins. Being clear on who you are (and who you are not) is the starting point of a successful free range career.

This is radically different to career-cage thinking. In the career-cage world, if someone doesn't love what you have to say, then that's a problem. The aim is to keep the peace, keep your head down and generally glide through the day and come out, you know, okay.

In the free range world, the opposite is true. So much so that years ago I opened up a fresh document and wrote the following words as a reminder for myself:

If you don't love what I have to say, here's what I want from you:

★ I want you to hate me.

★ I want you to say, 'that girl is not funny'.

★ Say 'Her fees are too high. What, she doesn't even offer regular, structured coaching? Who does she think she is?'

★ I want you to say, 'Her language is unprofessional. She flaps her hands when she speaks. Can't *stand* her.'

★ *Then, I want you to tell your friends how much you can't stand me.*

★ When you run out of ammunition, tell them I have really bad hair.

Hate is similar to love. The person or brand you hate gets under your skin. They hit a sensitive spot that is beyond apathy. You feel something inside you start bubbling away. If someone hates me, no hard feelings; I'm just wrong for them – maybe just for now, maybe forever. Whatever. But the fact that someone can be incited to hate me means that my message is clear and strong enough that it will get under the skin of someone else. Someone who will love my message, and feel I am speaking directly to them. If that's you, my message will hit a spot that is beyond apathy. You will feel something inside you start bubbling away... And that's a life-changing experience.

Scary stuff huh? But this might be the one thing that makes the difference between you shining... or failing.

Using the usual please-everyone approach, it takes just a few bad comments to topple your dreams. Aside from having an average, struggling business, when you pander to the beige-est common denominator, you end up unhappy: you end up trying to be someone you're not.

You know what? *Screw that.*

This is not about those people who don't get it. They were never going to become customers or loyal fans anyway. Pandering to them will just make you more average, more insipid and take you further away from the life you imagined. And the truth is, they won't love you, no matter what.

For every person who laughs at you when you are at your brightest, someone else loves you for exactly the same reason. The key to standing out and getting paid to be you is choosing those right people, and speaking to them and only them, in your full voice.

For example, Benny Lewis's language-learning approach has come under fire from the traditional language-learning community:

My approach is different to most linguists online. I am not interested in speaking the language perfectly, or becoming a literature expert. I want to get the learning over as fast as possible so I can go have fun on travels, and that's what my people want too, but it seems to offend the traditional experts.

They kind of hate me, yet that has helped me. All these bloggers who dislike what I do will write about me and link to me: 'Benny is an idiot because... link'! So they send traffic my way. They have helped expand my readership by not liking me!

The result is that Benny has one of the most popular online language learning blogs in the world, a blog that earns him a full-time living.

In the next chapter you will see more on how choosing your people and appealing only to them gives you the edge to rise above the competition. For now, though, let's focus on you. You see, this Third Way is not about following someone else's rules and playing someone else's game. This is about living life on your terms.

So, think of your free range idea (or ideas!) and the people you'd love to deliver them to, and consider this:

★ What would you say to your people if you weren't worried about rejection?

★ What possibilities would you create if you weren't worried about being 'odd'?

★ Who would you be and what would you do if you were not afraid of other people's laughter?

Above all, tell me... *Who told you you'd be loved more if you were someone else?*

Big lives come from bold steps

I know you are reading this because you want something more in your life. You want to do something meaningful and have a fabulous life in the process. The problem is, if you are holding back then there is no way of making this happen. Molly Mahar, life coach and author of the *Stratejoy* blog, explains:

When we want to do something more or bigger *but are held back by fear of putting ourselves out there, we are going to be trapped in a cycle of unfulfilled desire.*

When we care too much about what others might think of us, we're not going to make the changes or take the risks that are necessary to put our brilliance out in the world or simply be comfortable in our own skin.

Result? We stay stuck.

And that sucks.

The part that sucks most is the thought that you might let other people's world view hold you back from doing your own thing.

The freedom you're looking for doesn't come with a simple business plan. It comes when you take a deep breath and choose who gets a say in your life... and who does not.

My journey from bland to bold

Reading back over this I can see you might get the impression this is only a path for brave people with boundless self-confidence. It's not. *I know this because I'm the biggest people-pleasing approval-junkie out there.*

Want to know how I, a chronic people-pleaser, came to this place?

Unsurprisingly, I started out trying to appeal to 'as many people as possible'. I chose a wide niche (choosing them because I thought they were a 'smart business choice' not because I really wanted to work with them). I toned down my language to sound the way I thought I was supposed to. I deleted anything that might be off-putting to my harshest critics (who were mostly made up of the frowning committee of inner critics who tut tutted in my head).

As a result, I ended up creating something that people thought looked 'very nice'.

Problem is, 'nice' doesn't pay the bills, and nice doesn't nurture your soul and your need to do something meaningful with your life. 'Nice' is code for *inoffensive* and *I am sure someone else will like it* (but then, no one ever really does). Watch out if someone says your idea is *nice*. It means you're probably not going to sell much.

This wasn't the life and freedom I had envisaged when quitting my job.

I had a choice: look nice, stay in the middle, while holding myself back from being me, or take a deep breath, focus on a small group of people I care about, and have the guts to stand out.

One guess which one I chose.

You got it. And I haven't looked back since. I have no doubt that had I not got up the guts to say *no* to the parts that felt wrong and *yes* to the parts that felt right (but that some people might laugh at) then I wouldn't be writing this today. I'd have given up the dream, gone back to a job with a failed business, a cynical outlook and old hopes of freedom, dashed.

It's not enough to have an idea and quit a job. *True liberation comes when you quit the shackles that you put on yourself.*

And that's how we stand up, stand out and rock out your life.

20 HOW TO DECIDE WHO GETS TO GIVE YOU MONEY

'The key to my success is I write to a specific audience (niche), and know how to find them.'
John Locke (who sold over a million fiction e-books without a publishing deal)

If you are not going to appeal to everyone then who *do* you want to appeal to? That's an important question.

As we learned in the previous chapter, when you try to please everyone then you end up pleasing no one. Here's why this is. To please everyone, you have to leave out the good bits, the parts that spark and grab people. *Go generic and everyone will think your brand is nice, but no one will think it is for them.*

Imagine you are starting out as a massage therapist. Who do you want to appeal to? Say 'everyone' and the next question will be, 'how?' Your answer might be 'I'll give good massages for reasonable prices.'

Congratulations. You are now competing with every massage therapist in the world.

Almost every person starting out in any industry says their point of difference is 'good service' and 'lower prices'. These days 'I'll treat you like an individual' is a popular add-on. If everyone offers these three as their point of difference then do you really think they are unique? No. Those three points have become *expected*.

If you want to stand out you need something more.

Most people can only think of 'service' and 'price' as their differentiators because those factors are the only ones that appeal to *everyone*. If you aim for everyone you are 100 per cent right: you need to do more work for lower money as that's the only way in the crowded mass market.

Hmm, lower income for more work. How is that idea chiming with the life you want to create? Competing on price is a non-starter. For one thing you can be undercut all too easily. Someone offers your service a bit cheaper than you and you'll have to eat into your profits (read: lower your salary) to fight back.

The middle of the road is the most dangerous place to be (that's where you get run over by fast-moving traffic).

Going back to the massage business, what would happen if instead of *everyone* you targeted full-time mums who need a break? Or time-poor professionals who crave pampering *in their lunchbreak?*

When you choose niche, you can start to differentiate what you do. For example, the mum-niche could make their place child-friendly (or child-free even!). They can tailor packages to the mum market. They could speak about the situations that mums will be in that would lead to them needing a massage. They can talk about the guilt you might feel spending time and money on yourself yet how much better you can be for your child if you take that hour out for yourself. They could start a newsletter about self-care as a mum. *They could end up writing a column about the topic in their local paper.*

Of course, *everyone* wouldn't get this approach, so you'll miss out on the builder down the road who has a crick in his back from heavy lifting. But that will be more than made up for by the fact that your niche will flock to you.

That builder down the road had no reason to go to you if next door's massage service was cheaper: your mums do. If you don't specialize, you'll end up competing on price and then the only way is down.

Get this right and your people will go to you above anywhere else, then come back and tell their friends.

With a niche you rule the world. Specifically, *your niche's* world. You attract customers you love being around, you gain confidence (sorry Great-Aunt Maude, you might think my business is a bit *out-there* but you're not my *niche*), and you stand out. Result: more customers, more money and more satisfaction.

From burnout to brilliant: a real life turnaround

Grace Marshall became a coach while juggling life as mum of two young children. With sleepless nights and years of overwhelm behind her, and a coaching qualification and love for helping people under her belt, she decided to launch herself as a life coach specializing in burnout.

When I first met Grace she was working under the brand 'from burnout to brilliant', which she describes as 'for anyone who was feeling burned out. I didn't want to leave anyone out so I included everyone who might experience burnout be it mums or teachers or doctors or preachers.'

Full marks for choosing a specific topic area – burnout – but without a niche of people, Grace's message was fragmented:

My website had a big list of burnout issues for everyone from students to professionals to grandparents. I kept thinking 'they might be looking for X so I should put something on there about that!' No one bought my first offers because no one knew what I was about.

Grace took some advice and looked at niching further:

I realized I really wanted to speak to parents who had been through what I had been through. So I niched down to parents and burnout. Then I niched further to mums who were running their businesses.

Every time someone signed up to my email list I asked 'What's your biggest challenge in juggling business and family?' And the biggest was time: how do I find time with kids – that was the biggest topic.

Grace responded by launching her first productivity programme for mums in business – *and it filled faster than anything else she had offered.* Since then her business has grown more than ever before.

*It's funny, I resisted specializing in productivity for a while
because I thought I'm not a time management guru! But people
kept asking me how do you do it, how do I fit it all in?*

*I got to thinking, I was running my business, a full-time mum
to two young children, attending a leadership course, involved in
the community, running a networking group for mums in my local
area and still having quality time with my husband and kids at
the end of the day. Maybe I did know a bit about finding time!*

*Now my productivity brand is that I'm not that organized
super-mum type – far from it – but I need to get things done
just like you, so here's how I've learned to deal with things.
That appeals to people who are not naturally organized;
they get that I know where they are coming from.*

Remember the all-rounder myth (Chapter 7) where we think we
have to be everything to everyone and resist the parts we do best?
That's what was happening here. When people are asking you for
help and you're saying 'no I'm not good enough to talk about that',
pay attention: your natural specialization and a great niche might
be lurking beneath that.

Fear of niching

The three biggest resistances to niching are: 1) fear of missing out
on work; 2) fear of being 'mean' by excluding people (particularly
difficult for natural helpers!); 3) limiting yourself. Grace was held
back by all three:

*It was difficult for me to niche, I didn't want anyone to feel left
out, I didn't want to miss anyone's business and I didn't want
to miss out on variety. The funny thing is that when people start
working with me I end up covering all the issues in the sessions
anyway, so I'm getting more variety than I had before... and
more work as well.*[4]

By excluding people you end up reaching and helping more people
than ever.

How to choose your niche

First notice the wording: you don't find your niche, you *choose* it. The truth is there is no one perfect niche out there waiting for you. Choose your niche based on what you want and what you love right now, then tweak it to fit, free range style.

Many people think a niche is like those demographic boxes you tick in a survey. So they might say 'my niche is women aged 25–45 (and maybe some men too)'. That's not a niche – that's the bulk of the purchasing population! What about their attitudes, their habits, the binding factors that mean they would probably get on if they met at a party? Attitude defines a niche as much as anything else.

Choose a niche for you

Quite possibly your first niche will be a group that is currently experiencing a problem that you have faced, or the sort of people with whom you have spent a lot of time. It is easier to communicate with people whose situation you truly understand.

Once you have an idea who you'd like to work with, describe them. What makes them different from the average person who would buy this product or service? What is their interest in your topic? Who are the people you don't want to work with? Be as descriptive as you want here. Remember: you are talking about real people, so get into the nitty gritty of how they think and feel. A rule of thumb is that you should never describe your niche with the words 'anyone who'. 'Anyone' is not a niche; get specific.

Make sure you are excited about working with these people. If you choose a niche purely on 'shoulds', such as 'I should work with corporates because they have the biggest budgets' *but* the thought of working with corporations makes your blood run cold, don't do it!

Much like the struggling person who came to me saying he wanted to target 'rich people' because they had a lot of money: turned out he didn't know any 'rich people' and didn't feel comfortable hanging out with anyone who earned an above average salary. No wonder he wasn't getting very far. A 'hot market' is not hot if you don't know anything about it.

This doesn't mean being stupid, by the way. If your niche market is broke and can't or won't pay, then avoid it unless you want to end up the same way. But don't assume you have to hit the top end of the market to make a great living. If you love your niche, can speak their language and they can pay... you're off to a great start.

MINI CASE STUDY

I was so stuck for the first six months because I felt I had to work with anyone who would give me money for my services. It meant that I had only two paying clients (for whom I did work I didn't really enjoy, for vastly reduced rates). However after doing a Free Range Humans course I chose a niche I love, gained oodles of confidence, learned shed loads about marketing, started selling beautiful logo designs, added over 50 new designs and services to my shop and have seen my business grow steadily. Not bad with a breastfed baby under 1!

Gemma Regalado-Hawkey, Southampton, UK
www.janeandphilbert.com

Once you know who you want to work with, the next question is: how are you going to present yourself to them?

21 HOW TO BRAND LIKE A ROCK STAR

'Find out who you are and do it on purpose.' *Dolly Parton*

I was going to open this chapter with examples of fabulous rock star brands and what we can learn from them: such as how Lady GaGa grabbed the most successful female recording artist mantle by shunning the usual boxes, doing her own thing and creating just for her ultra-loyal tribe.

But there are hundreds of articles on that already. To me, there is a more interesting part to branding: a quieter part that most people don't talk about. And that is this simple truth: *branding like a rock star takes guts.*

You don't need 10 million Twitter fans, your tribe's name tattooed on your arm, or an over-the-top music brand to brand like a rock star. But you do need the guts to not blindly follow the herd. And that's the opposite of what you've been taught to do in career-cage land.

Surrounded by pressure to be self-effacing and fit in, when it comes to explaining who you are and what you are about in your business, the temptation is to squish down the message that is bubbling up to spill out and replace it with a message that feels more acceptable. Fitting in and toning it down may sound like an easy route to success but nothing could be further from the truth. Follow the herd, and your powerful roar can dwindle down to a mini mewl.

Branding like a rock star means more than a logo or a gimmick. It means coming out of hiding, stepping up and being you in shining lights.

The power of branding as you

A great example of the power of coming out of hiding is Jenny Jameson, a free range graduate. Jenny has gone from frustrated employee in a cubicle, to a one-woman powerhouse, tackling the multimillion-dollar diet industry head on.

A chronic yo-yo dieter since her teens, Jenny realized that diets were doing her life more harm than good:

> All my life, I thought I couldn't do the things I wanted until
> I lost weight. For years I told myself I don't deserve this
> promotion, or that success, because I'm overweight.
> I sometimes wouldn't want to meet new people because
> I thought they would think I was too fat. It's such an awful
> mindset and it had nothing to do with being healthy.

So, Jenny stopped dieting, stopped weighing herself, and in the process changed her life. She finally did all those things she was putting off doing until she could 'fit into those stupid skinny jeans'. Now Jenny shows women how to ditch their diets and do the same (without eating the fridge). A brave mission, but that's not why I'm sharing this story. I'm sharing it because this story almost didn't happen.

Jenny's first brand name was Zero Gravity Life. 'I came up with Zero Gravity Life when I was still in a job,' she explains, 'I thought a good brand had to be something witty and clever. I thought I had to not offend people; I didn't want to alienate anyone and this name sounded nice. So launched quietly as Zero G.'

Turns out that wasn't the greatest plan.

> No one really got it. It just wasn't exciting anyone – not my
> niche, and not me. I was struggling to get any interest. Plus,
> it might be a nice name, but it didn't feel like me.

Jenny quickly found the brand name was running the show and she felt like a lowly employee (in her own one-person company):

> I knew what I wanted to say but I kept having to ask, 'does this
> fit with the Zero G message?' If you have to check with your
> brand 'is this alright?' then your brand is wrong. I didn't go free
> range to have to check for permission before I speak!

So Jenny took a deep breath and after a few months under Zero Gravity she rebranded to *F*ck the Diets*. Which does pretty much what it says on the tin. In this new brand, Jenny is angry – angry *for* you, not at you; she is raw and honest and says it like it is. With the motto *ditch the diet and get a life* she is roaring her support of you living your life right now, without waiting to drop a dress size or look the way magazines tell you that you should. And that's basically Jenny unleashed:

> When I changed brand I gave myself permission to start saying these things in my own voice; people really started to respond and get it. My follower numbers have more than tripled since I became F*ck The Diets. More opportunities have opened up than I ever imagined possible.
>
> Sure I lost a few people who didn't like this new style, and I understand that, but that's nothing compared to the growth explosion that has happened since. Now I'm reaching more people than I could have when playing it safe.

Your brand is more than a name

To me the most important part of Jenny's story is not the name change. That was the catalyst that gave her permission to be who she really was. However, had Jenny just changed the name and kept all her content the same (ie safe and bland) then none of these successes would have happened.

You see, a brand is every single experience that people have of you. From, yes, your brand name, but also what you say, how you say it, what you offer, how you offer it, who your 'people' are. The feel of the experience – are you about inspiration, education, seriousness, lightness, setting off a flare and shining brightly or toning it down and existing gently? How do people experience you, and how do you respond to them?

A good example of this is Ms Cupcake's brand. The focus is passion, fun and old-fashioned *generosity*. Generosity comes across in the bold colourful website, the warm welcome at their stall and shop, and most importantly, in the cakes themselves. The first thing you notice about her cupcakes are their generous size: oversized creations with miles of beautiful frosting.

'I know most people can't eat one of my cupcakes by themselves,' Melissa explains. 'Most people share one, and that's part of the experience of Ms Cupcake. The brand is big, fun and generous.'

Many people see branding as false or misleading, but good free range branding is the exact opposite. A great brand takes what you have to offer and puts it on the outside so people 'get' you and your offering, even before they buy from you.

Having said all that, your brand name is the first impression people have of you. It is also the ongoing image people hold of you and it will impact on what you do. Here's how to choose yours.

EXERCISE   **Seven steps to choosing your first brand name**

1 Write out a list of 20–30 words that describe what you are really about.

    I put this challenge to a client running a relaxation and alternative medicine practice and he came up with words such as 'authenticity', 'calm', 'change', 'renewal' and 'fresh'. Some of those words are obvious to his field, and others are a little more personal to him as a person.

2 Review your list. Now, cross out any words you put there because you thought you 'should' (hint: those are the words everyone will be using), not because they are really, really core to you.

3 Shortlist. Write your favourite three to five words at the top of a page with a column underneath each one.

4 Brainstorm. Under each word, brainstorm brand names. Don't edit, just write ideas as they come. You are looking for something that captures both the feel of your approach and personality as well as being immediately understandable to someone who hears it.

5 Sanity check: is this 'too smart' or 'wonderfully sticky'? A great brand name should connect with your audience the moment they hear it (ie be 'sticky'): you should not need an 'About' page to explain it before people get it. That was the problem with Zero Gravity Life: it took a while before the metaphor sunk in (in zero gravity your weight doesn't matter!). It's fine to have hidden meaning as a secondary benefit but if your niche doesn't connect with the name immediately people won't stick around to get the rest of it.

▶

◄

6 Personality check: is this really you? Are you happy going out and being this person? Remember: there is no such thing as a good brand name. There is only a brand name that is good for you. Choosing a name purely because it sounds clever is like choosing a shirt because it is trendy and looks good on the model – but when you put it on it makes you look terrible. Your brand should not make you feel you have to be someone you're not. If you're not happy being that brand you'll hold yourself back.

7 Be prepared to change your brand name. You may have noticed that I said your *first* brand name. That wasn't a mistake. Your first brand name will probably not be your last. The truth is that most people play with a safe option before finding their true voice. The biggest insights will come on the ground.

Remember, you don't have to spend a million dollars rebranding. I rebranded my business for the price of a few lattes.

As you get into motion then your true brand – name and all – will emerge in a way you can never achieve thinking from the sidelines. As Jenny says, 'I'm glad I didn't wait for the perfect brand name before I launched, I would never have found my perfect name if I hadn't been out there doing this for real.'

TIP   **Why you don't need a fancy logo**

You can have a great brand without a bespoke logo. I have seen people waste months choosing a logo: yet when was the last time you bought something just because it had a clever logo? A logo is the last thing you should be worrying about in your first few months: write out your name in a decent font and get going. You can always come back to it when you're actually up, running and profitable.

If in doubt, take inspiration from Deloitte. Their logo is just their name written in a regular font with a dot at the end – and that hasn't stopped them being one of the biggest consultancies in the world.

22 HOW TO STAND OUT FROM THE CROWD

'If you don't get noticed, you don't have anything. You just have to be noticed, but the art is in getting noticed naturally, without screaming or without tricks.'

Leo Burnett

A little story for you:

When Cathy was 14 years old she was desperate to be an individual. She didn't want to be just one of the herd, so Cathy made an effort to dress differently. She wore her hair shorter, her clothes looser, her jewellery bolder. Problem was, outside of her social group, no one noticed. To adults, she was indistinguishable from the rest of the 14-year-old crowd. Sales assistants treated her just like everyone else. Cathy got more and more frustrated – and no one wants to see a frustrated teenager!

One day, in art class, her teacher asked everyone to write out a paragraph describing their own personal style. Cathy wrote: 'I don't follow trends. I wear my jeans looser than Sara's, my hair shorter than Ramona's and my jewellery bolder than Bella's.'

Cathy's teacher read this, and wrote the following comment: 'If you truly don't follow trends, then why did you use what others wear to define your style?'

That was when it hit Cathy. She had been following trends: she was following them to define who she was not. Her jeans were not like Sara's; her hair was not like Ramona's; her jewellery was not like Bella's. But she had no idea how to describe herself without reference to other people.

Cathy would never stand out as a real individual when her only approach was 'to do something a bit different from the crowd'.

This is the story of a 14-year-old girl. It is also the story of almost every new business that says *I want to stand out from the crowd*.

There are three factors involved in standing out from the crowd

FIGURE 4.1

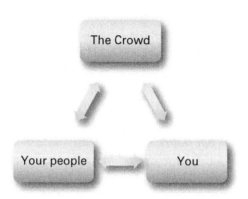

The crowd means your competition. *You* means you personally, your brand, what you offer, what you say, and how you communicate. *Your people* means your niche, or more simply: the people who you want to buy some of that great stuff you have to offer.

When you think about standing out from the crowd, where do you start? With the crowd, with you, or with your people?

1 Most people start with the crowd.

2 Most people start by looking at their competitors as their very first step.

3 Most people struggle to stand out for this very reason.

When your website is a copy (with minor variations) of someone else's, when your language is 'industry gobbledygook' (like every other struggling business), and when other people's products, services, attitudes and prices define what you think you are 'allowed to do', then you are behaving like Cathy. You are *always* defined by someone else (often, ironically, by someone else who is struggling). Start from the crowd, and your business runs a high chance of being a pale copy of everyone else's.

Big business makes this mistake too. A trend in recent times has been the search to create the 'iPhone killer'. A few years ago, I worked on a consulting gig for a mobile handset manufacturer with this very aim. They wanted to create the iPhone killer but they hadn't come close. We were taken on to help figure out why. Like a good consultant, I delved into their research, read reams of paper filled with every competitive analysis, market trend, focus group write ups... Then, after weeks of getting bogged in the minutia of this trend, that territory, that projection, it became blindingly clear to me that the truth was much simpler: the problem with the iPhone killer is that it can't.

The iPhone killer is always referenced by the iPhone. Improve a few features and add on a doo-dad that the iPhone is lacking and yes, you may raise sales for a while. But then the iPhone will come back and lap you with something spectacular and game changing. Then you'll have to start again.

I want to create the iPhone killer is a very different statement to *I want to create the best (or best-selling) mobile handset on the market.* The first statement guarantees you will stay mediocre. The second statement gives you the potential to truly innovate, on your terms. The second is closer to the way the iPhone got created in the first place.

How to stand out
(by being more you)

Don't start with 'the crowd'. They come later, once you have something to say and someone to be. For now, start with two factors: you, and your people. Your aim is to be the most attractive to that sliver of society who you really want to work with.

You don't need a radical new idea for this. You simply need to embrace your 1 per cent.

The 1 per cent / 100 per cent model of standing out

How different do you think you need to be in order to stand out? Do you think you need to be completely new and fresh? Have a new niche no one else is touching? Pioneer a new field?

That sounds like a lot of hard work. What if, instead, you only had to find your 1 per cent difference?

The 1 per cent / 100 per cent model is an approach I designed to articulate the large impact of small differences.

I was discussing this idea with a friend over coffee and our choice of meeting place illustrated this perfectly. When I am buying coffee from a chain, I always choose Café Nero. Why? Well, it's not just that they do good coffee:

★ It's that they use real freakin' chocolate in their hot chocolates rather than synthetic 'chocolate flavouring'.

★ It's the fact that they always have two jugs of water on the counter, next to a stack of fresh glasses, there for you to help yourself.

★ Real chocolate. Free water. That's what I call a 1 per cent difference.

However that 1 per cent difference gets 100 per cent of my business. When you're a small business, 100 per cent of someone's business is excellent. Start thinking of your people now. What are they really buying when they buy what you are thinking of offering? (hint: it's not just the coffee).

What 1 per cent difference will equal 100 per cent of their individual custom to you?: 1) it might be the language you use – you're far more friendly / professional / informal / intellectual / down to earth (delete as appropriate) and that resonates with the niche we call your people; 2) it might be that your brand feels more 'kick ass women' rather than 'soft, pink and girly'. Or vice versa.

Whatever it is, there are two rules on making the 1 per cent difference work for you.

Rule 1: you need to be 1 per cent different on something that the people you are comparing yourself against *don't* treat as important

Seth Godin puts it well:

> *You don't get someone to switch because you're cheaper than Walmart. You don't get someone to switch because you serve bigger portions than the big-portion steakhouse down the street... Instead, you gain converts by winning at something the existing provider didn't think was so important.* [5]

I bet that other coffee chains don't think a constant supply of water and a certain type of chocolate is that important. And they are right too – it's not crucial for them or their people. It won't stop someone dominating the café market and having their own loyal fans.

But these details are a 1 per cent difference that will convert 100 per cent of that type of person who does find it important, and that's enough of a market for a whole other business.

Here is how to get this result for yourself.

Rule 2: your 1 per cent difference should come from YOU

Defining your identity and brand by comparison to that of your competitors is not what I am talking about when I say find your 1 per cent difference. The 1 per cent / 100 per cent model is about identifying the points where you are *naturally different* and breathing life into them so they become bigger and clearer.

So, are you an image consultant who is approachable and warm or super-efficient and bluntly honest? Are you an image consultant who kicks butt on women's corporate wardrobes or changes the lives of dads whose cupboards are packed with clothes they wore 10 years ago (but who have nothing to wear today)? Do you make me feel sexy or relaxed?

There is no right answer – only the truth about who you are versus the person you think you should be.

Remember:

★ Standing out is not a gimmicky add-on.

★ Being outstanding is not an afterthought tacked on by a marketing department.

★ Putting your best self out there is the most generous thing you can do for the world. *Hiding is not a contribution.*

MINI CASE STUDY

You were 100 per cent spot on about me hiding my *self* from the business idea. I took myself to a café and wrote out a new version based on 'if I was brave and had the courage of my convictions'. The end result is something with far more pizazz and people are really taking notice.

Anna Samson, Devon, UK

You don't have to be a certain type of person to succeed in your industry. Is your product that much more advanced or is it simpler? Are you the one who hugs people better or the one who goes 'bang' with the raw truth? Whatever the answer, don't hide it. That's your secret superpower.

TIP   **Who am I again? (the problem with personal branding)**

When we talk about 'identifying a really-you 1 per cent difference' or 'creating an authentic personal brand' an interesting question arises: who *are* you anyway? There are a dozen versions of you that bubble up in any one day. One moment you feel serious and analytical and another you feel playful and irreverent. Which of these personas is the 'real you'?

The answer: all of them.

A more useful question is: which *version* of you do you want to be in your business? 'Authentic' does not mean 'show up and act the way you feel on the day, one moment being sunny and the other shouting at everyone and the other having a strop'. Unless your personal brand is to be wildly unpredictable, this is not a great move.

▶

A great personal brand means taking a certain aspect of your personality and putting it on speed.

For example, my friend Phillip Van Nostrand is a photographer. He is also a wonderful human being. As a natural people-person Phil quickly makes his subjects feel at ease. The result is beautiful, natural shots that capture your personality. As one of his clients says: 'His whole breezy charm thing won us over, and it shows in the pictures! He had our group relaxed and happy, and I loved that he was able to capture the "moments" – the quiet ones, the sweet ones, and the hilarious ones.'

Phil's 1 per cent difference is that he is the friendly photographer who makes people feel good about themselves with an uplifting experience on shoots... and he delivers photos that capture your personality. This is also what you might call his 'personal brand'. Whatever you call it, playing to this strength is part of the reason Phil managed to quit his job as a teacher, and build up a successful photography business (in a crowded market).[6]

Of course, Phil is far more complex than that description, in the same way that I am sure you are more complex than any two-paragraph summary! But the point is, he has made that aspect of who he is key to his 1 per cent, and now you too have the freedom to choose which parts of *you* get to shine the most brightly.

The free range approach is all about embracing the *inimitable* you. Standing out means taking what you might sometimes see as weaknesses or setbacks and, instead of stuffing them into a box and pretending to be someone else, turning them into advantages. That means placing the real you and your real message at the fore of what you do, and inhabiting that version of you throughout your business.

That is when you truly stand out, free range style.

Remember: if you are struggling to pick out your stand-out points, a simple shortcut is to do a good personality assessment as outlined in Chapter 7. When you understand your personality in detail it is far easier to hone in on your 1 per cent differences!

FREE RANGE PROFILE CONNIE HOZVICKA – 'I EARNED MORE IN ONE MONTH THAN I DID IN THREE MONTHS IN MY JOB'

Connie was an art teacher who dreamed of being a 'real artist'. She loved her students and the opportunity to inspire their creativity, yet the admin and bureaucracy that went along with her teaching role left her feeling drained at the end of each day.

On the drive to work – her favourite 30 minutes of the day – Connie would imagine what it would be like to be able to spend her days creating, connecting with other artists and moving around at her own pace in places that inspired her. Of course, this was just a dream. Connie had always been told it was impossible to make a living from art. Art was what you did on the side of a real job.

Then, Connie moved across the country. As she didn't know many local artists she started up a little blog as a way to connect with other artists. That blog was *Dirty Footprints Studio*.

Back then, every Sunday I'd be sitting on the couch wearing my pyjamas thinking I don't want to have to go to work tomorrow. I had my laptop out and loved working on Dirty Footprints... but I kept thinking I have to have health insurance, I have to have all the benefits I get as an employee, I just have to work.

It was in the evening, as the sun was setting through the window, I felt like I was watching an egg timer – every Sunday on that couch, how long do I have. How long until Monday, how long until summer break, it was all one big countdown until my spare time where I could live my real life.

Around this time, Connie also got into art journaling. She decided to share her personal journaling process via YouTube videos. Turns out not many others were doing YouTube videos on art journals at the time, and art journaling was a hot topic. So her videos became popular and sent a lot of traffic to Connie's blog.

Connie didn't expect this outcome, but once it happened she made the most of it. While still in her full-time job, she created a blog series called '30 Journals 30 Days', interviewing 30 well-known artists on their own journals. Connie published the 30 interviews as blog posts. At the same time, she was launching her first paid online programme: 'Art Journal LOVE Letters' – so, to promote it, she placed a PayPal 'buy' button for the course at the bottom of each of the 30 interviews.

'The 30 artists that I interviewed sent their followers to my website to read their posts,' Connie explains, 'combining that with the YouTube videos, my numbers grew massively.' As a result, little newbie Connie completely sold out the first live round of her online programme (and the ongoing version of the programme ended up selling more than 300 places). 'That made me think, hey, maybe this can work!'... But still fears of an unreliable income held Connie back.

That summer, Connie ramped things up a notch. She launched BIG, her fearless painting online adventure and: 'It sold well. Really well. Within one month I'd made more money than I would make in three months as a teacher and I loved every minute of it'.

The first BIG course launched on 4 July.

On 6 July, Connie quit her job and went free range.

Today, Connie runs *Dirty Footprints Studio* full time – for a while she was selling her art (ending up with 48 commissions in one year) and she now focuses on inspiring and helping people to tap into their own creativity as artists. She paints every day, is still doing fascinating partnerships and her courses are so popular they often sell out before public announcement:

I don't know what day it is half the time! It's one amazing big blur. When I stopped looking for something to fall back on that's when I fell right into the thing I was meant to be doing.

Keep in mind that when she started out, Connie was still working full-time, leaving the house at 7.30 am every morning.

> *It was hard work, don't get me wrong. I was working on Dirty Footprints in every spare moment I could find: writing, videoing and running courses, and of course creating my own art. I was even trying to sneak it in at work. I knew I wanted to make this happen more than anything.*

Connie didn't have advantages or contacts. Everything was built up using her passion, gentle enthusiasm and the approach I call the Free Range Faststart. In the next chapter you are going to learn how to apply this Faststart approach for yourself.[7]

23 HOW TO DO THE FREE RANGE FASTSTART

'You can't stay in your corner of the forest waiting for others to come to you. You have to go to them sometimes.' *Winnie the Pooh (A A Milne)*

This chapter is a shortcut to zooming your way into traffic and your first pay cheque using one simple system (and a touch of charm). Best of all, if you get this bit right then you can forget your search engine ranking.

I mean it. Using this approach, you can build a six-figure business without worrying about your Google rank or paying for an ad.

When researching this book I discovered something interesting: the people who break through consistently do one particular thing (often without realizing it). *This thing was the single biggest differentiator between the businesses I know that got off the ground fast and the ones that struggled for years.* Want to know what it is?

Meet the Free Range Faststart

The Free Range Faststart is three simple steps that let you reach a lot of your niche at once.

Before doing the Faststart you might be feeling like the new stallholder who has landed the smallest and quietest stall at the market. You're in a corner with no one walking by. No matter how nice you make your stall and how great you make those offers it makes no difference: no one knows you are there.

Meanwhile, you're watching another stallholder with a long queue of your ideal customers who are laughing and talking with him. And most of all, buying. How frustrating!

Now, imagine that that same stallholder offers you the chance to join him for a while and get known by those people. You jump at the chance.

You want to be where the traffic is.

But it's not just about the traffic. You quickly discover that the more established stallholder's inclusion of you on his stand is an implicit recommendation: those people in the queue are already smiling at you, saying hello. The ones who ignored you before now trust you, because of who you're with.

Yes, they'd love to get on your mailing list, yes they'd love to hear more, and they can't believe they never heard of you before because your product is just what they were looking for.

No matter you were only around the corner before, they just didn't know to look for you. Now you're on their radar big time. That's what happens with the Free Range Faststart.

Faststart in practice

A few years ago, Rachel Winard was an attorney working a high-stress job in a corporate law firm in New York. She suffered from lupus, a condition that reacts badly to stress, and after years of trying to survive her long days (with 4 am starts) she finally quit her job for the sake of her health. As she looked for something to bring in an income, Rachel's friends and family encouraged her to launch her own hand-made soap line, using the recipes she had been making herself for years – the result of not being able to find anything on the market that worked for easily irritated lupus skin.

So, she pulled out her soap recipes, got herself a 'virtual shop' on Etsy.com 'and that's how Soapwalla was born, late one night, in my small apartment kitchen,' Rachel explains. However, once she launched, the burning question was *how will anyone hear about me?* Friends advised her to hire an expensive marketing firm; however, Rachel ignored that advice and decided to do it herself using the Faststart steps below.

It was through this approach that Soapwalla got traffic, gained loyal customers, and ended up being featured as a must-have product in the *New York Times* style magazine (without Rachel ever writing a press release or contacting a journalist).

Here are three steps to do it for yourself:

How to do the Free Range Faststart

Step 1. Identify a list of people or organizations in your field who have the audience you are looking for

When Rachel launched Soapwalla, she reached out to form connections with other established blogs and websites where she felt:

> *The people were on the same wavelength as me. I did a lot of searches on who I thought would be a good fit and picked out people who had similar goals to me – natural beauty, simple, wholesome. Websites such as* Fig and Sage *and* Well and Good.

Lesson: there is little point casting around trying to reach one individual at a time when actually, someone else already has hundreds or thousands of your perfect customers. Your first step is to identify who those 'audience holders' are.

Step 2. Make contact and build a relationship

Rachel's next step was to get in touch with these website owners.

> *I introduced myself to the people I identified. Sometimes they would respond and sometimes they would not; I formed friendships with the ones who replied, and it went from there.*
>
> *For example, there's an eco-friendly products blog I like, called* Petite Planet. *I emailed an introduction, explained my product line and shared my story of why I got started and what my ethical principles were behind the production of my products.*
>
> *The owner of* Petite Planet *responded and I got to know her; we built up an email relationship and I mailed her products to try. She tried something she liked and put a post on her blog telling my story in a condensed version. I remember I jumped up and down for five minutes when I read that first review. It was really reaffirming that this was what I was supposed to be*

doing. Since then I've built up friendships with other blog and website owners. That's how I've got all my press.

Lesson: even when you have identified where your perfect customers are, few people are keen to let you leap in and start pitching to the audience they have spent years growing and caring for. Get to know your potential Faststart partners first, and then look at how you can benefit them.

Step 3. Exchange mutual value

In this step you make an offer of mutual value to you and your Faststart partner. The value you are looking for is to tap into some of that stream of audience that they have. The value they get in return might be content for their website, or your assistance with part of a project or event.

Rachel offered up her personal story – of creating Soapwalla as a result of years of searching for a product that would work for her skin condition – as content for the bloggers and website owners she got friendly with. She also offered free samples to her new contacts, which is the physical product version of linking to a relevant article on your website (ie giving free content to prove your quality).

Lesson: don't sound like an advertisement. Be personable, think from the perspective of this other busy person, and don't ask to get paid – if this person holds the audience you are desperately trying to reach the biggest payment you can get is to get exposed to their people.

For another example of how this process works, in one of my own Faststart partnerships, I started by offering a guest post on a website, then I became a regular poster. Soon I got to know the people behind this website, met up in person and through informal conversations, realized I could offer assistance both in terms of a) developing some strategies they needed (and which I knew about from my previous career) and b) by providing some services that their audience were begging for, but which they didn't have the resource to provide themselves.

The result was that we partnered and launched an event: they provided the people (which I sorely needed at the time!), I provided the service and we both got benefit from something we could not have done by ourselves separately. Plus, I got exposure to a large list of my niche, who then joined my tribe, all from a standing start.

I had no introductions, no contacts, no status and no reason for this to work other than the fact that I took the Faststart steps: *first understand their needs, offer something of value, then get to know them better (by really listening) and offer something that will work for both of you.*

These three steps can take you from unknown to being seen by tens of thousands of people in your niche, with the bonus of a tacit recommendation from an authority those people already trust. Much smarter than handing out one business card at a time, right?

There are many variations of the three steps; your faststart offer might be as simple as offering a guest blog post with a link back to you at the bottom (this is also the best way to raise your Google ranking!) or in fact, showcasing them first, as Connie did in her story.

Attitude alignment: ask the right question

Right now you're in an amazing position. Thanks to social media you can now follow anyone and send them a message (even if only 140 characters!) without getting lost in an inbox or asking a gate-keeper for permission. Thing is, so can everyone else. However, there is something you can do to show you are different from the shouting hordes.

To stand out from the crowd in your Faststart, make sure you are asking yourself the right question:

The question is not just 'how can that person benefit me', the bigger point is 'how can I benefit them'?

Look, I know you wouldn't run up to a stranger on the street, grab them by the lapels and shout *let me market to your people!* So let's not do that online. Focus on them, on their needs and what you can contribute. Remember there is no rule that you must be offered, well, *anything* in return for your support or time, so only do what you would be willing to do for free anyway. Always consider *would I want to have coffee with this person if I wasn't going to get anything out of it?*

BONUS ARTICLE

How to meet people without feeling sleazy

You just 'don't do' networking meetings? I'm with you! Here are some human ways to meet people you actually would enjoy spending time with (and one big mistake to avoid): **http://frh.me/meethumans** To go straight to this article, scan the QR code with your smartphone or tablet.

Choosing your Faststart partners

Here are three different types of Faststart partners (I have illustrated these using the example of guest blog posts but you are free to use different approaches).

1. Different from you

A person or organization that covers the broader topic in which you have a niche. For example, a women's personal fitness website would be a great place to focus if you offer personal fitness during pregnancy. From their perspective, you add value by coming in with a specialization that will chime with a portion of their niche, but which they haven't yet covered in much detail.

A variation is to guest-post on a blog with a completely different topic to yours, and focus on reaching your niche within that audience. For example, Benny of *Fluent in Three Months* says:

> *I don't write on other language blogs. You can guest-post completely out of your niche; just combine the two topics and put a relevant theme on it. On J D Roth's* Get Rich Slowly *website (a financial-themed blog) I did a post on how to learn a foreign language without spending a cent (in the US, language learning is associated with high cost so that played well). On Leo Babauta's* Zen Habits *(a minimalist and simple living blog) the post was on the* simple *way to learn foreign languages. The 20 per cent of readers interested in learning more about what you do will go to your site.*[8]

2. Multi-author blogs

This is a good one to focus on for your very first guest blog posts. Multi-author blogs are websites that provide mostly guest-post driven blog content (ie there is no single main author). Some popular examples are *Huffington Post*, *Copyblogger*, or other more niche examples. A more mainstream version of a multi-author blog is a magazine on your newsagent's shelves! Multi-author blogs are a better place to start as they are always looking for new content. Plus, the popular ones can get you better exposure to your niche than would most magazines.

3. Your direct competitors

I prefer to call competitors 'comparables': just because you're similar doesn't mean you have to fight it out. More often than not there is room for co-promotion, collaboration and many bonding sessions over coffee! *Connecting* rather than competing can lead to the richest and most rewarding relationships.

MINI CASE STUDY

Since coming across the free range approach I am much more open to trying out new things and seeing where they go. A friend and I set up a local co-working event and as a result have met some interesting people, and fun collaborations are starting to grow. For example, four of us are going to do a project together for a local hotel – it's pet friendly so we're going to make a walks video and then promote it on YouTube and a mobile app. Before, I would never have imagined this project happening, I thought this was stuff that 'other people' do – the more experienced, more successful, more well connected ones. But now I'm doing it!

Charlotte Davies, Cumbria, UK

TIP **Share your story**

Sharing your story is not essential to the Faststart. However, if you have something to share it can certainly help you on your way.

For example, people were keen to profile Rachel because she had a story to share rather than a pitch saying 'buy my stuff'! In the same way, knowing her story is also more appealing for buyers who know Rachel understands their situation:

My story lends my products credibility – the products have to work for my sensitive skin and I did years of research and honing and formulating and reformulating. I'm crazy particular about how I source raw ingredients and products. It's not just talk and that helps a lot. I really understand what people are going through.

In contrast, I have seen so many people tuck away their most interesting story, their real motivation, in an attempt to look modest or 'fit in' to the typical mould. That is a big mistake.

▶

Status is reassuring

I like the fact that my doctor has a degree certificate on her wall. It's comforting. That certificate is a reassuring sign saying *I know what I'm doing.* Usually you don't read every word on the certificate. You might not even notice it's there. But your subconscious certainly notices and treats this person differently.

When it comes to your situation, the primary job of status is to *extinguish the fear* that may hold back your potential clients (or collaborators) from taking you on. The secondary job of status is to *raise your value* so you can charge what you are worth.

Here is how to build that status much faster than most people imagine.

Status hacking 101

When I started out in a new field I was as status-free as anyone else. I went on a status campaign to change that:

★ Within a few weeks (before even quitting my job) I had delivered seminars at universities.

★ Two months in and I was published on some of the most popular websites for my niche.

★ Three months in and I was quoted as an expert in a book, and profiled in national press.

★ Six months later, I'd not only got a popular organization in my new field to take me on with an exclusive contract to run classes (ie guaranteed access to my niche) but they offered to pay me for the privilege... even though others were lining up to do it for free. I was also being asked to give talks at events I previously just watched from afar.

The outcome? I had the confidence and credentials to get the work I wanted at the rates I needed to charge. Again, this wasn't luck, it was just down to combining the Faststart with a simple 3-step approach to zooming up the status ladder.

All of the techniques in this chapter are based on a simple concept. Most people think status is a solid, immutable fact, an impenetrable fortress. It is not. Status is simply people's *perceptions* about you.

When you delve into these perceptions they turn out to take a pretty predictable form: pull apart any 'about page' that makes you think someone has status and you'll see the same building-block patterns again and again. Once you understand these predictable building blocks of status, and suss which status indicators have the biggest impact, then you can skip the years of trial and error and replicate them for yourself.

Three pillars of instant status

These building blocks fall into three categories:

FIGURE 4.2

Association, Publication, Quality: the 3 pillars of status.

Here's what they mean and how you can create them for yourself:

1. Association

The way we take in the world is informed by associating one thing with another. We see a young guy driving an open-top Porsche and without thinking about it, assume he is well-off. Of course he might be a struggling student borrowing the car from a friend in order to take her dog to the groomer... but if we were to stop and think of every conceivable explanation for every single thing we see, we would never get past our front door. So our brain makes shortcuts: guy driving Porsche = rich. That's how we get through the day.

Your niche take in the world in exactly the same way. So, what are they using to make assumptions about you? That's what status by association hacks in to. Status by association is when you associate yourself with something that already has status in your niche's eyes. That status-giver could be a household-name brand, a prestigious venue, an academic institution, a profession or background, or anything else currently holding status. Remember, right now your niche don't know who you are, and to help them get comfortable enough to want to find out we're going to have to give them something familiar and reassuring.

Here are some ways to get status by association in three minutes, three days or three weeks:

ACTION

Three-minute status-by-association hack:
you can get instant status by association by drawing on what you have in your life right now

For example, Helen was starting afresh as a hypnotherapist specializing in stress reduction for professionals. She didn't have any connections in that field and was afraid she would have to start at the bottom. However, she was coming out of a 10-year career for some well-known household-name brands. Helen didn't think this was relevant as she had never worked on 'stress' in these roles, but working with her she quickly saw that there was a link:

after a 10-year career working for [Very Big Company, Name You Would Know], and with directors of start-ups, I have witnessed first-hand the impact of stress, and discovered the most effective ways of...

Can you see how this has more impact than just writing, 'I'm a new hypnotherapist making a career change so hire me!'

▶

I know one seven-figure-earning speaking trainer whose personal brand revolves around being a former medical doctor. No one imagines for a moment that her medical background has any relation to her current work – but it lends immediate credibility.

You don't need a big company, institution or profession linked to your name to use this technique. Another quick win is numbers: how many countries have you been to or worked in? How many kids do you have (if relevant to business!)? How many books have you read on the topic? Is there anything in your own explorations that is status-giving? For example, did you attend teachings by any big names you care to mention?

Those are just a few examples. Get creative. You are not 16 years old, so you will have some status, somewhere, even if you have never worked in this field before. Identify that and put it out there to reassure your people.

Three-day status-by-association hack: this option lets you borrow someone else's status.

Find some friends, or friends of friends, who have – or are associated with – status that most of your niche would recognize. Offer them a freebie.

For example, if you're trying to get going as a coach for creative types, the line 'coached creatives from companies such as Twitter and My Space' has more impact than a full page of text. A testimonial from one of these people is even better.

Three-week status-by-association hack: give a talk at an institution, event or famous venue with status that your target clients will recognize.

Before I quit my job, I decided I needed some status. So, I made a list of everyone I knew with university connections, and of every institution I figured I could contact myself. Then I chose a friend of a colleague who worked in an academic institution that was quite forward thinking (so was more likely to take up my offer!). I presented myself to the relevant person and highlighted the parts of my background I knew would interest him. I made the offer to run some seminars there on a specific topic, just to get some experience and pass on some free insights to his students. My offer was accepted. Within a week I was able to edit my 'about' page to say 'delivered seminars on this topic at a university', all before I quit my job.

2. Publication

I remember meeting someone at a party who had recently taken on an image consultant. 'She was expensive,' my new friend explained, 'and I had to save to afford her services, but I figured if I was going to do this I should just go for the very best: *she's a published author and has been featured in the press and everything*'.

See what happened there? Status by publication (in a book and magazines) was correlated with being a leader in that field. We think: the magazine 'chose' them ergo they must be good. Luckily, you don't have to wait to be chosen in order to get some of this publication status goodness. Today, you can pick yourself.

TIP   **Pick yourself**

Today, we are at a point in history where more than ever you can pick yourself. Traditionally closed industries such as publishing, television and business are opening up to people who break the rules and make things happen. You don't even have to quit your job to take the first step.

Take writing a book, for example. Almost every person I know who got a non-fiction book deal in the last year – including me – got their deal when they were approached by a publisher as a result of their blog (or in a few cases, a free e-book that was spreading around the Internet). This makes sense: with more and more people producing and publishing online why take a bet on someone who just *claims* they can write?

Even better it's becoming more and more attractive to self-publish, meaning you really and truly don't need a gatekeeper to let you in. For example, did you know that anyone can publish straight to Kindle and get a listing on Amazon alongside hard-copy books?

Alternatively, publish yourself online. Guest posts can be a quick win to status. Identify potential websites to host your pieces, using the techniques in the Faststart section. The difference is that you are now choosing your host sites based on the status they convey. My client got a slot writing as an expert for the prestigious *Huffington Post* within a month of starting her

▶

business. She identified her own niche, and her own status using the techniques in this book, and then building on these stepping stones approached them directly and was accepted.

You don't have to go down the writing route. If you prefer live interaction, get known as the person who runs a regular 'go to' event for people in your niche. Go to a website such as Meetup. com – a website filled with people looking for live events to attend in your area – and launch your first informal event. Your first one might get five people in the pub (with three of them being your friends) but keep going, every month and soon you'll be able to say you're running 'Newcastle's only monthly event for over-50s adventure travellers'.

As a bonus, if your aim is to get quoted in magazines or newspapers, you'll find that having a platform such as one of the ideas above substantially increases your chances of being picked. Bottom line: don't wait to be noticed before you start; start so that you get noticed. By deciding to start your thing, and putting it out there, you get good and get known and people come to you: much smarter than waiting to be picked, 'just because'.

Here are some resources to get going without waiting to be picked

* Start a blog for free **www.blogger.com** or **www.wordpress.com**

* Publish a book straight to Kindle **https://kdp.amazon.com**

* Get your own radio show online **http://www.blogtalkradio.com/**

* Launch a mini event to a group of eager people **www.meetup.com**

* Advertise an event without a website **www.eventbrite.com**

MINI CASE STUDY

I always loved writing about travel and international issues but the idea of being a published travel writer was a bit of a fantasy. I'm a 30-year-old with a regular job, I thought, why would anyone publish *me*?

One day I started a blog. I worked at it for a while, not thinking anyone was reading it, but writing nonetheless. This year my piece on travelling as a single woman in Morocco got picked up by a Lonely Planet website. After that, I took a short evening class in travel writing, and then pitched a piece to *The Guardian* newspaper. I suddenly found myself published in *The Guardian*'s Travel section, writing about the top ideas-festivals around the world!

It's a revelation that you just do things and then other things happen. I know that sounds obvious but really, it's amazing how much comes from just doing.

Kim Willis, London, UK, **www.borderskipping.com**

MINI CASE STUDY

I had a 'good job' as an HR manager in the fashion industry. But I always thought that I should be doing something, you know, a bit more amazing than working in an office. In my late twenties I was still waiting and hoping that someone would come along and pick me... but when I eventually started picking myself magical things began to happen. I crystallized my message, developed a website and subscriber list in less than three weeks... all without any previous techical experience at all! Now I've quit my job and left the career-cage world.

Hattie Brazeley, London, UK[13]

3. Quality

You can usually tell if someone has status by the way they present themselves. Quality is simple: have integrity, deliver great work, and care for your people above all.

As Ms Cupcake says, 'We are fun and flirty but above all, a premium brand. I'll throw away a whole tray of cupcakes if the quality is not perfect.' That dedication to quality contributes to her well-earned status.

Quality perception backs up this dedication to quality. That means: no random ads cluttering up your website side bar, no broken links leading to a Coming Soon page, and using a nice, clear picture of you on your social media profiles and your website (not that blurry one your friend took in the pub, even if it *is* the best photo of you, ever).

Finally, remember that no one wants to dine in an empty restaurant. Don't do yourself down by hustling desperately for one client... That just tells the world that others don't want what you have to offer, which definitely doesn't suggest high status. In contrast, one newbie I know would leave empty spots on her courses rather than hustle for the last dollar. That paid off because she got the reputation of always selling out, of being in demand, and consequently that became a self-perpetuating belief. Soon her courses *were* selling out. That's the power of quality perception.

From dream list to real life

Jenny of *F*ck the Diets* used these techniques for herself. When she was a participant on one of my courses a year ago, she completed an exercise asking who you would want to be associated with in the future.

Last week Jenny sent me a message:

I just went to an event where one of my biggest heroes walked up to me and said; 'Are you Jenny of F*ck the Diets?'

I couldn't believe she even knew my name. A year ago in your course I wrote down her name and thought, maybe in 3 or 4 years I might be brave enough to go up and introduce myself, but today she walked up to me!

Then, this week, Jenny followed up with more news:

You won't believe it, but the editor of my dream magazine emailed me and said I'm welcome to write for them. I didn't ask – she offered! I've never been paid to write in my life, and I'm being published!

To be clear, Jenny is not a brash extrovert by any means. She is an introverted, thoughtful woman – far more likely to push you into the spotlight than try to grab it for herself. She would have been the last person to believe she would be profiled as an example of status-building.

That is precisely why I have chosen to share her story. That someone who is *not* a natural self-promoter by any means can make this happen, primarily through the passion and quality of what she is putting out there, and gutsy action she has taken, is testimony that anyone can use these techniques and make them their own.

Jenny's advice:

What did I have to do? Go out there, meet people, be myself and be nice. Offer to help with no thought of reward. Publish posts even when that felt uncomfortable and scary. It was all simple steps, but you don't just push a button. Trying again, again and often... that worked.

Forget the idea of starting at the bottom. Instead, start at the top and then work your way up. The bottom may be crowded, cramped and competitive, but Free Range Humans know that just means the top is wide open and waiting for you.

TIP   Do it for real. You're looking to build a reputation and, as Henry Ford said, 'You can't build a reputation on what you say you're going to do.' Every time you take action, hit publish, make that phone call, you are taking another block to build that reputation differentiating you from the scores of people who just talk about their ideas.

DOS AND DON'TS

Dos and don'ts of getting press

DO specialize. Journalists like quoting specialists. A counsellor whose website is about the topic of handling anger will get more press enquiries than someone who bills themselves as a generic counsellor.

DO respond fast to press enquiries. Journalists usually have short deadlines and are likely to take the first responses.

DO be clear, concise and quotable in your responses. And always keep in mind the sort of reader that reads that publication! Make life easy for the journalist.

DO use **http://www.helpareporter.com**. Then, do respond to the emails as soon as they hit your inbox – the fastest responses have the best chance. And DO change the subject line.

DO follow the #journorequest tag on Twitter. This tag is used by journalists looking for people to feature, and experts for stories. Follow it and respond.

DO target the right people (ie: specific journalists) if you *are* going to contact them directly. *Every time you find an article you'd have liked to be quoted in, take the name of the journalist and start a list. You can often find that journalist on Twitter and form a connection.*

DO get personal. *For example, if you have just started doing Etsy.com over 50, look for the over 50 angle. If you have overcome something related to your area personally then you can be a case study and move into being an expert from there. Think outside the box.*

DON'T do what every other beginner does (ie: send press release after press release to generic email addresses, and then give up when it 'doesn't work').

▶

DO send a short, clear email with everything they need to read in one or two paragraphs.

DON'T just send a link to your web page and expect them to trawl through it to find the one interesting titbit they might be interested in! Value their time if you want them to value you.

DON'T disregard trade publications (eg: specialist mags for a particular industry) – you'll have an easier time getting quoted as a stress expert in an accountancy magazine than in *Psychologies*. You never know who will pick up a magazine that is lying about, and you never know if the journo who is writing that piece for the small magazine is a freelancer who might also work for your dream publication.

26 HOW TO COMMUNICATE IN AN UNSUCKY WAY

'If you can't explain it to a 6-year-old, you don't understand it yourself.' *Albert Einstein*

Something strange happens when some people start describing their business. Within the first sentence, the Confusion Genie lands in their path. The Genie takes out a wand and a spell is cast in which simple, tangible ideas become general and meaningless.

For example take this clear idea:

I declutter your home-office space so you can actually see your desk – and show you quick and super-simple ways to keep it that way forever.

versus

I employ a range of innovative and goal-specific techniques to remove extraneous physical build-up and realign your domestic work environment with your personal and business goals in the short and long term.

Whaaat? (It's okay, I didn't get it either).

I'm sure you've heard something like that before. Frankly, most business communication sucks. Big time. This is a leftover of the 1980s style that author Hugh MacLeod calls *Dinosaurspeak*:

Ninety-five percent of marketing talks to us in Dinosaurspeak. This style of marketing lingo *was pretty universal a few years ago, which in Internet time was like the Mesozoic era...*

But now, thanks to the Internet, markets have become smarter and faster than the companies that service them; language has changed and Dinosaurspeak must face extinction. Of course it does.

Talk like a human being, not like one of Stalin's apparatchiks. People are hardwired to respond favourably to that.[14]

The very first thing most people do when describing their business 'officially' is to remove their personality and their real thoughts from their communication.

Dinosaurspeak removes the heart of so many potentially fabulous business ideas. That second declutterer above, the one who tried to look smart and 'professional', forgot that when you get down to it, their clients really, honestly *want to be able to see their desks and stop feeling so overwhelmed about it all.*

In the process, they failed to communicate the service in a way that resonates with the client. Or, in human-speak, *their description sucks.*

Ironically, this attempt to look businesslike removes the very factor that is core to the success of any business – namely, *speaking the words that are in the clients' heads.* I seriously doubt that anyone is waking up in the middle of the night thinking, 'Oh no! I have to sort out that extraneous physical build-up and realign my domestic work environment with my personal and business goals! I hope someone shows up with a range of innovative and goal-specific techniques.'

More likely it is: 'That darn desk is overflowing with papers, I can't find anything and my partner won't stop nagging me about the mess. Gah, too complicated to take on right now!' Listen to what they are thinking and speak to that.

Speak human

As Dan Pallotta wrote in the *Harvard Business Review*, 'when I was younger, if I didn't understand what people were saying, I thought I was stupid. Now I realize that if it's to people's benefit that I understand them, but I don't, then they're the ones who are stupid.'[15]

Using abstract buzzwords in place of meaningful language is not a new phenomenon. George Orwell spoke about it in his 1946 essay 'Politics and the English Language'[16] where he spoke out against what he saw as a 'mixture of vagueness and sheer incompetence' in contemporary writing. Orwell identified three main problems:

The writer either has a meaning and cannot express it, or he inadvertently says something else, or he is almost indifferent as to whether his words mean anything or not...

As soon as certain topics are raised, the concrete melts into the abstract and no one seems able to think of turns of speech that are not hackneyed: prose consists less and less of words chosen for the sake of their meaning, and more of phrases tacked together like the sections of a prefabricated hen-house.

That essay could equally have been written about sucky business-speak today. In an attempt to look professional, meaning gets stripped away from many business communications. Here's how to do things differently.

First get the words *right*, then get the word out

A common question asked by people starting a business is 'how do I get the word out there?' My reply is, 'that's not the right question'. The best marketing techniques in the world mean nothing *until you have meaningful words to get out there*. There is no point reaching a thousand people if they don't connect with what you have to say. You'll lose all that investment you put into getting noticed as no one will stick around!

To avoid this mistake follow three simple principles:

1 first understand (what people are thinking);

2 then get the words clear (so you are speaking the language they are using in their own heads);

3 then get it out there.

You don't have 20 minutes to describe your business to each person who might be interested. You have a sentence or two in which they will either get it and love it or nod, smile and go away. So let's make those sentences count.

Practise using clear language even when just brainstorming ideas yourself. The way you speak about your business to yourself is crucial. If you were the confusing declutterer above, it would be very easy to lose sight of who your customers were, what they really wanted and what you were really providing. That's when a previously great idea gets mangled and fails.

So, when describing your business – be it face-to-face, in a 140 character Twitter message, or on your first website, ask yourself, 'Is this what I *really* mean?'

Are you choosing words for their meaning, for their imagery and the feelings/ideas they evoke? Or are you choosing them because 'that's just what people in my industry should say'? If so, go back to basics and explain it in a way that a 6-year-old would understand, then grow from that. Finally, write all your communications as if you were writing to a particular individual.

That encourages you to speak like you would to a human (not a 'prospect'). You'll know you've got it right when people respond by saying things like:

★ 'I'm so relieved, I thought I was the only one who thought that!'

★ 'Did you write this for me?'

★ 'Are you living in my head?'

★ Often followed by 'Do you take cash or card?'

In contrast, use Dinosaurspeak and the usual response is 'that's nice, I should check you out sometime' (code for 'hmm, I wonder what's on TV tonight?').

EXERCISE   Four steps to unsucky communication

Be a language detective and listen to your niche. Don't feed them the words you think they should say but listen to what they *actually* say.

If you have ever been in the position your niche are in now, then try this exercise now (if you have never been in their position, do this exercise after spending time with your niche and actively listening to them talking about your topic):

1 Take a sheet of paper and write out the exact words you said to yourself when you were back in the situation that

▶

◄

you are helping them with now. For example, if you are a voice coach helping new voice-over artists build the skills to get commercial gigs, back when you were that budding voice-over artist, you might have said 'I really want to get into this but I don't know who to call or whether my voice is even good enough!'

2 Get specific: did you use any particular phrases when you were thinking about this? For example that voice-artist might have thought 'maybe this is just a pointless dream. It feels like a closed shop where you only get jobs if you're on the inside.' Write yours down.

3 Now go for gold: was there anything you felt or thought that you never dared articulate to anyone else? Something about fears, or dreams, or something too silly to say out loud? Write that down and circle it, highlight it, stick gold stars on it. I guarantee you are not the only person to have felt or thought that.

4 Once you have identified words that resonate and remind you of how you *really* felt back then, write a paragraph description of what you do, and who you do it for, giving these words a starring role.

As Orwell says, good communication uses 'language as an instrument for expressing, and not for concealing or preventing thought'. Anyone can slap down some Dinosaurspeak. It takes a bit more thought to speak human, but it's a language well worth learning.

Inspiration

For a more lighthearted look at this topic, check out **www.unsuck-it.com** which describes its purpose as 'unsucking your douchey business jargon'. Plug in one meaningless phrase and get a real-world translation in return.

Or visit **www.plainenglish.co.uk** whose gobbledygook generator can create a meaningless jargon-filled phrase at a touch of a button.

27 WHY YOU DON'T HAVE TO BE AN ALL-ROUNDER
(you don't have to do it all alone)

'To be yourself in a world that is constantly trying to make you something else is the greatest accomplishment.' *Ralph Waldo Emerson*

As we've been covering all these strategies, I'm wondering how you've been feeling about doing them in practice. I know when I was starting out I would read books and think 'that's a great idea!' and then get bogged down on the implementation. Sometimes this is just because it's a new concept: there's a bit of a learning curve, and then you'll be fine. But in other cases, it's because an approach requires you to do something that really doesn't play to your strengths and you know it isn't ever going to go smoothly. How can you handle that situation?

Let's go back to Peter Shankman who we met in Part 3. You may think ADHD could be a drawback to running a business but Peter begs to differ:

Look, I screw up my appointment calendar all the time: things like booking two dinners on two different continents at the same time! I actually did that once, can you imagine? So now I have an assistant who keeps track of these things for me.

But even before then, when I was doing it all myself, I still managed to keep things going. I'm not special – everyone has a weakness. Find ways around it and accentuate what you're good at.

In other words, focus on your strengths and manage your weaknesses. This is core to free ranging. Out of the career cage, there is no prize for showing up and slogging away at work that doesn't get results and that you don't love. Here are some ways to get the best results (while loving what you do).

Strategies to match your strengths

One way is to choose the correct strategies for you. You can follow the strategies of top business gurus in the world, but if those strategies are out of line with your personality I can guarantee they will flop. There is no point trying to build up your business based on going to networking parties five nights a week if you are a solitary type who does better with the written word (and vice versa). You might certainly get something from those 'out of flow' techniques but they will never be the main reason you shine (plus, you'll hate it).

This explains why there are so many different books out there each giving seemingly conflicting advice: advice that worked for one profile might not work for another. Good news is, when you know your personality profile it is much easier to hone in on which strategies to follow, which successful free rangers to check out, and easily focus on exactly what you need.

Some of my favourite personality profile assessments for this are here: **http://frh.me/personalityassessments**

MINI CASE STUDY

I was trying to set up an Internet-based business and struggling. The free range approach encouraged me to take a step back and look at where my strengths lay. I am a supportive person and I get the most from collaborating with others – so little wonder I wasn't doing well all by myself! As a result, I started to look for like-minded people I could hook up with and I met up with a lady who runs a holiday *finca* (estate) in Spain. Long story short, it turned out to be the right move. We have workshops and retreats planned for the next six months and I am teaching weekly yoga there too. Since I started to follow my strengths many opportunities have presented themselves and I am really excited about where I am going.

Helen Hooper, Mijas, Spain (formerly UK-based)

Share the love

Another way to play to your strengths is to delegate. Don't get me wrong. In the early days you will do most things yourself. At first 'I'm my own boss' just means 'I sweep the (metaphorical) floors, as well as meet the clients'. Do it, keep notes on how you did it, the mistakes you made and what you learnt. But then, when you're off the ground, you can – and should – get someone else to do the parts that are most out of flow for you so that you can focus on where you add the most value.

In the free range world, getting help does not mean taking on full-time employees. You can either collaborate with others or hire 'virtual' assistance.

Collaborations

As you get off the ground, you can do joint projects with other people in your field who love doing the parts you hate (and vice versa). Start these collaborations informally, experimenting with just one project rather than signing a lifetime deal! Meet people using the approaches in Chapter 23. Once you find the right partnerships, working with others can be one of the most fun and rewarding ways to fund your free range life.

Outsourcing

Alternatively, you can hire your own assistance online. For example, for one-off freelance, websites such as Elance.com or PeoplePerHour.com have a range of people offering out as many skills as you can imagine. I have used these services for website projects that would have taken me days to learn from scratch. Alternatively the quirky fiverr.com is a place you can get a range of small tasks done for $5. I found my transcriber for this book on there – she transcribed my audio dictations at the cost of $5 for 15 mins.

MINI CASE STUDY

I discovered how easy it was to maximize my abilities by outsourcing my inabilities – allowing me to do things more quickly. For example, I have outsourced artwork for an upcoming adult colouring/activity book. I had the idea but do not have the necessary artist skills so I am using an artist in Spain through GURU.com!

Michael Mentessi, Essex, UK

Generally if a task only needs to be done once, hire someone from these sites. If it needs to be done repeatedly, it's time to explore a virtual assistant. A vitual assistant (VA) is someone who works for you for a certain number of hours per month and can be based anywhere. Your VA can help you with the tasks that take up too much time or headspace or simply don't fit your strengths. This can include answering emails, taking care of clients, social media, research, technical assistance (eg website updates or sometimes even design) or just helping organize you. What they offer depends on the VA.

You can get a low cost VA from about £10 an hour. However I find that unless you have a lot of patience and are willing to micro-manage, the time taken to communicate with a VA from some of the big offshore companies can eat into the time-saving benefits.

I prefer to use a native English speaking VA who is either free range themselves, or part of a smaller, high quality team. A decent VA will cost you anywhere from £15–£50+ an hour. The difference pays off. My VA responds to all client enquiries, takes care of any technical fixes, and often sits down with me to figure out logistics of courses (somewhat important when I say things like 'I seem to have promised 30 people personalized gift packs by next week!'). More importantly, she is a trusted virtual team member who brings some order to my wilder ideas.

However, don't get hung up on thinking you need a perfect VA before you start – in your first months you can easily get by by yourself, and if you need something specific you can grab one-off technical support quickly and affordably. But it is good to know you won't have to do it all by yourself forever.

For help finding the best people, I keep track of smart VAs and other technical helpers who work well with free rangers at **www.freerangegenies.com**

28 HOW TO SELL WITHOUT SELLING YOUR SOUL

'In the words of the philosopher Scepturn, the founder of my profession: am I going to get paid for this?'

Terry Pratchett, Night Watch

Imagine this: your brand is out there for real. Your website is up and looking mighty fine. You're getting Faststart connections all over the place. *You're smoking hot right now.* People are noticing you. Your ideal clients are coming your way and sticking around. *They want more of you.*

You could say the dating game is going well.

In fact, you've met someone special. You're so happy to have found each other – you were starting to believe it would never happen. You don't want to mess up this beautiful relationship you have going... but something is bothering you.

You both know that the S-word is on the agenda. That dirty S-word creeps into your mind every time you make eye contact. You are fantasizing about having your first S-word experience with them all the time, in private, but you never raise it in public (well, not without apologizing).

What if you get rejected? What if they slap you down? What if they tell you, 'I thought you were better than that?'

Okay. This isn't the nineteenth century, so let's put it out there. At the end of the day you're going to have to stop just flirting, look them straight in the eye and... *sell.*

Oh yes, I said the S-word! *Sales.*

In our culture we think of sales very much like the Victorians thought about sex: ie pretty often, but never spoken about in polite society.

Thinking that sales just isn't your thing? Trust me, you are not alone. I asked a few free range fledglings their views on sales and here is a selection of the results:

★ I just hate selling. I think it is a confidence thing and fear of rejection, but also not wanting to come across as pushy.

★ I want to make money but not if it means selling my soul.

★ Personally, I hate getting cold calls about products/services I don't want, so I'm really uneasy about doing it myself.

★ Sales? *It's just not me.*

You know what feeling uncomfortable with pushy sales means? It means you don't suck. Congratulations.

I honestly don't know *anyone* who loves cold calling and pushing crap on to other people! If I had to do that type of sales I don't think I'd be my own boss at all. However, that's not the only way to do sales.

Instead of selling your soul, try selling *from* your soul. Like this.

The four e's of selling without selling your soul

Guidelines for every Free Range Human to live and work by:

1. Enthusiasm

Why are you doing this again? Oh yeah, it's because you *love* it! You are *excited* about working with these people; you *believe* in the message. You *can't wait* to get started!

How about communicating *that* rather than trying to 'convince' someone?

If you find your enthusiasm for your subject mysteriously shuts down when you move into 'doing sales', consider how you would describe this were it *someone else's* product you were recommending to a friend who really needed it. Would you want to grab them by the shoulders and say 'do it man, do it for you!'? Capture that enthusiasm, that genuine care, and use this at the core of what you communicate.

When you truly believe in and love what you do, it doesn't feel like selling. It's sharing your enthusiasm and passion for what you're offering.

2. Engagement

Forget the idea of sales being those 1980s red-tie boys BS-ing their way to a commission. Free Range Humans do it *with love*. To do that, you need to get to know your niche, understand them, and above all, focus on helping them. Get in the habit of thinking from their perspective.

On a fresh sheet of paper, identify 5–10 benefits your client will get from taking you up on your offer. I don't mean the obvious features, for example 'a blue box with a ribbon' or 'three osteopathy sessions'. I mean what is the outcome? For example, 'relief at having got a winning gift for their partner (with little effort)' or 'no more lower back pain'.

Think of your benefits now: will your client get more energy? Get more done? Feel more confident? Have a garden that makes people say *Wow*?

HINT   list your benefits in the language your people might use when talking about this outcome to a friend. This lets you engage more closely with how they actually think and feel.

---

3. Equanimity

Equanimity: self-assurance and groundedness; or, not being pushy and desperate.

If you're coming from a position of thinking you might miss out, that people are out to steal your ideas, and that others in your field are competitors (rather than potential collaborators and friends) then this will come across in a whiff of desperation. When you look desperate, empty-restaurant syndrome kicks in, and people sidle away. End result: people don't buy what you have to offer.

Bottom line: you have to trust in yourself and your potential before others can trust in you. That's when you stop copying others in your field and start listening to yourself. That's when people buy from you readily.

4. Ethics

Ethics is really simple: treat others as you expect to be treated. That's what being a decent person is about.

That's the way I try to operate, from my personal ethics. That means: I don't take people on my higher-end courses if they have credit card debt. On any programme where there are applications I will turn down more people than I take on. I tend to give away more on my courses than people can do in one go, because I'd rather overdeliver than hold back.

That's my version of ethics – some people would go further and think that my version is *too* money-oriented. Others would think my ethics are way too touchy feely and not money-oriented enough. That's fine. We each come to our own balance based on our own values.

So I'm not going to tell you how to behave. But I will ask you to consider it yourself, get clear on *your* values, and *your* benchmark so that you won't be rocked at the last minute by thinking: 'Is this okay, can I say that?'

Free Range ethics comes from the premise that you only sell something that you believe is good. Every moment you hold back is a moment that someone who needs your product, service or ideas is missing out on getting what they need.

When you waver on selling, ask yourself *am I holding back out of genuine ethics... or are people missing out because of my own insecurities about being too forward?*

That's the big question.

TIP   **Sell like a shop (not a haggling trader)**

This is a tip for people delivering a service. If you are uncomfortable about getting on the phone and negotiating a price with a client, set things up so you don't have to ever have that conversation. The way to do that is *productize*.

This means, instead of saying 'contact me to talk prices', create pre-designed packages on your website, with a name for the package, and the amount clearly stated.

For example, a web designer could have the Simple Web Starter Pack that includes:

* a three-page website;

* loaded on to your server ready to go;

* a telephone kick-off session to show you how to edit it yourself;

* bonus: social media widgets already installed.

State the price as clearly as a shop would put a label on a product, and announce this as your recommended place to begin. *The majority of your starter customers will buy a package without negotiation.* After all, most of us don't haggle over products in shops, right?

Remember, your customers probably hate negotiating as much as you do: if your website or brochure says 'call me to discuss price' you are not only setting yourself up for an uncomfortable chat but also putting off a lot of customers who, like you, hate getting into that conversation knowing they will be 'sold at'.

29 GET COMFORTABLE WITH SETTING YOUR SALARY

Imagine that you had to come up with an extra £1,000 for an essential payment that has to be made in the next three weeks. Importantly, this is *above and beyond* anything you can pull from your salary or savings.

What would you do?

When you're in a job, your only option is to put £1,000 on credit; not exactly a sustainable habit! But it's one that most employees take. Indeed, when I was back in the career cage, dipping into my overdraft was a regular occurrence towards the end of the month (with the predictable blow-out on pay day). Since establishing myself as a free ranger, I haven't got into credit card debt once. I hear similar stories from other free rangers as well.

There are a few reasons for this. The first is that you are simply less likely to throw money around because you know how it was earned.

The second reason is that you can act as your own bank. For example, recently I was riding in a London cab with two other free rangers. One of them was visiting from overseas and had fallen into an unfortunate accommodation situation and we were escorting her to a different hotel. As she had already paid for her first hotel for the week, now she had to pay double in one of the most expensive cities in the world. Not fun! We made it our mission that by the end of the cab ride we would come up with a way for her to make that money back by doing something extra within her business. We brainstormed ideas and found three excellent, fun and easy ideas that she could execute in the next week. We turned this into an opportunity to create three times as much as what she 'lost', just by getting creative.

When you're free range, if you have to come up with that extra £1,000 *you have the ability to create that money from your head.*

If you need extra cash, then you have the freedom to launch a new service, promote an existing product, sell your time for a one-off project, or offer to promote someone else's offering.

Throughout this book we've been looking at creating a *life* that you love, and sometimes that can feel separate to the money question, but to me they are one and the same. I don't buy into this idea that there is some sort of nobility in being constantly short of money (with no way to fix it). Life throws curveballs your way; we don't know what is going to happen with ourselves or our loved ones, and *money means options* to take care of life no matter what.

However money-talk is new for most of us. We don't get encouraged to think about money in the job world: your boss sets your salary, money hits your bank account every month, and you don't have much control over how much you get. If you want more, you have to ask for it by negotiating a higher salary (hands up anyone else who finds salary negotiations uncomfortable!). Even then, you don't control what you get. In the free range world you do have control and it's important to get comfortable with the idea that you are allowed to make money and set your income level.

To do that, you have to know your money motivator. That means going back to what's important. For me, at the end of the day, it's not *really* about having nice shoes, or supporting my foodie restaurant habit (though they are important extras in my life). Ultimately, money is about the ability to take care of myself and the people I love, now and in the future.

For another free ranger, who is also a mum, her motivator is taking care of her son and daughter. She says, 'My kids were my main motivator for making the move to a free range life and they are the main motivator making sure I charge what I'm worth. When agreeing a fee, every £100 I compromise on is £100 that could have been spent on my kids. Show me a mum that will let a stranger take money from their children!'

Knowing your motivator is crucial to getting over that nagging voice in your head that says *am I allowed to charge more than bare minimum* or *if something feels fun shouldn't I just do it for free?* Yes, you can, and no you shouldn't, and your money motivator will tell you why.

To find your money motivator, get aware of your personal values: you may not value shiny expensive things, but you might value future security, or time away, or a good house, or something else. Whatever pushes your buttons, identify it, and remind yourself of that motivator every time you make a decision about how much to charge and what to put out there.

MINI CASE STUDY

The other day I hired my first photographer's assistant – part-time, just one day a week – and I was excited and nervous about doing it. I thought. 'Now I gotta come up with the money to pay him!' My friend suggested, 'Just raise your prices.'

So I gave myself a raise. I raised my hourly rates by 25 per cent and no one blinked an eye. I had an inquiry the next day, a theatre company wanting headshots, I told them my higher rates and they responded: *perfect.* How awesome is that? Now I can pay my assistant easily. Wedding photo-season is coming up, and I'm excited!

Phillip Van Nostrand, Santa Barbara, USA, **www.phillipvn.com**

DOS AND DON'TS   Dos and don'ts of pricing

DO be aware that most people undercharge (particularly for services).

DO charge at a level that lets you: 1) have the income you want for the number of sales you are likely to get; 2) feel enthused about delivering after they buy (rather than feeling like you're doing too much work for too little money).

DO realize there is no intrinsic price point for a certain product, service or period of time. For example a one-hour coaching session can range in price from £20, £200, £2,000 and I've even heard of a coach who charges five figures. All for a one-hour session.

▶

◀

DON'T set your prices by looking at the competition and trying to undercut them by a few pounds. Competing on price is never a smart strategy if you're a one-person band. You compete for the people who don't want to pay (ie the toughest and most time-consuming customers). And you can get undercut at any moment. *Undercutting works for supermarkets because of their size. You are not a supermarket.* Competing on price alone is a quick route to failure for a solo-preneur.

DO get creative: what else could you add to your offering that doesn't cost you more of your time, but does increase the value for your customer?

DO deliver value. Every time. If in doubt ask yourself *if the customer gets the results they are looking for from this product/service will they think it was a good deal?* That's what you're shooting for.

DON'T assume people will always look for the cheapest price. There are several studies showing that the cheapest wine on a restaurant's wine list is not usually the most popular. Indeed, while I love a great deal, several times I have turned down providers and products for being too cheap: I unconsciously equated low price with low quality thinking 'there must be something wrong with it at that price'. Trust me, your customers will think the same way.

30 WHAT TO DO WHEN YOU GET STUCK
(when to give up and when to give in)

This book is mostly about starting, and let's face it: starting is exciting. But what happens when you hit a wall?

Which, by the way, you will. There will come a point – about halfway through your project – when you are tempted to give up. You will tell yourself you made the wrong choice and maybe you just can't do it right now. This is not a bad thing. Sometimes, resistance is feedback: perhaps you are trying to do something against your personality, and need to change your game so it does fit.

But sometimes, resistance occurs because *that's just what happens to everyone*, halfway to the finishing line. When you feel that block you need to know two things: when to give up, and when to give in.

When to give up

★ When it feels so unnatural you can't bear to do it – *give up*.

★ When you feel like your soul is writhing in a cage – *give up*.

★ When the idea of actually doing that thing fills you with dread – or boredom – and you'd rather go to sleep – *give up*.

Okay, so that idea was not the right one. Change the idea; morph it into something that gets you excited.

However, when you simply lose focus and daydream more than you do the work – give up... for a while. Take a walk, work on something else, sleep. Come back tomorrow. But whatever you do, don't give up on your mission. Find another path to bring it into being.

★ If you can't write today, then grab a recorder and audio it instead.

★ If you can't find the words, draw a picture.

★ If that isn't happening, *change the damn topic* and create something that feels right.

Find a way that works, for you, and do that one. Now.

When to give in

There is a difference between *wrong choice* and *fear*. Don't confuse the two. With a wrong choice, apply the above: change the game and try another strategy. With fear (which often hides under the mask of wrong choice) don't give up – instead, give in.

Fear happens, all too often, at the point of momentum. When you move into your flow, *where it feels like you're losing control –* you will think: 'Wait, pull up, this isn't part of the plan. What if it goes wrong? What if it's not the best option? What if they laugh? *Is this allowed?'*

When you feel that way, DO NOT STOP, dive right into the loss of control, dive into the fear.

Do not check Facebook. Do not click away. *Dive in. Headlong rush. Past the comfort zone...*

And hello flow.

You know you hit flow because time flies, and momentum builds and control is out the window. When momentum hits, push through. Stay up later, work that much more intensely, get it out the door bigger and better, do more and be more *and don't let anyone tell you that is not OK*. Ride off the thrill of the buzz of being the full and present you, who shines so brightly when you are doing your thing.

Every creator, every person with a mission, everyone who is doing something that feels so good knows the feeling of flow.

Flow is that moment where something (that is not your left brain) takes over the pen and writes for you.

Flow is where you solve, in 10 minutes, a problem that others have struggled on for days... and afterwards you ask *how did I know to do that?*

That right there, that's flow. Sexy, seductive flow. And I'm addicted to it like creative crack.

Here's how to score your flow:

1 **Create**. Push. Hard. Do not wait for flow; it comes to those who start. You want to write? Write every damn day. You want to find something that you love to do every day? Get out of that house and doing something you love. Anything. It doesn't matter what. What matters is that you moved into its path.

2 **Listen**. To what is and is not working while you push it. Listen well, and dance with the changes. Learn to identify the moments of flow – they will be the ones where you want to stop because it feels a bit too much – those are the moments to lean in deeper.

3 **Respond**. To what is not working. Change it up. Stop writing, start talking. Stop talking and start making. Stop thinking about the Reasons Why Not and start listing to the reasons why. Stop thinking by yourself and find another perspective. As they say: *if you do what you've always done you'll get what you've always got.*

4 **Feed your soul**. The best moment comes when you're about to fall asleep after hours embroiled in the tangle of your creation, papers everywhere. You thought you hit your limit and you had to give it a rest. Within minutes your mind stills and the answer comes. Bam. Flow strikes.

    Float in the ocean, walk in the park, sleep. Do those things that feed your soul. Then, go back to step one and create your heart out.

I spent years fighting flow; I shed tears of frustration thrashing about in my self-made box labelled 'the person I think I should be', hell bent on doing it *just the way it looks in my head.*

Before I met flow, I thought the words 'give in' were for weak people. And then I discovered I was wrong. Giving in is not giving up. It is simply letting go of the handrail and freewheeling your way down that very right path... which to my surprise is down a road labelled 'get the hell out of your own way'.

RESOURCES

Resistance often shows up as procrastination. If you're a chronic procrasinator check out this video on productive procrastination: (really, check it out *now*. If you put it off the irony would be unbearable) **http://frh.me/procrastinatemore** To go straight to this video, without procrastinating, scan the QR code NOW with your smartphone or tablet

TIP

Take your creativity seriously (you get out what you put in)

John Maynard Keynes said that there is nothing more disastrous than a rational policy in an irrational world. He was talking about economics but the principle applies as much to creativity. Sure, you *should* be able to come up with great ideas and the best solutions by sitting in a white-walled room staring at a screen. But really, if that's not working, then it's not rational to keep pretending it is a good idea.

Take your creativity seriously, and put yourself in the best position to think outside the box. For example, in the early days of my business, I was stuck for weeks with no idea how to move forward. I hadn't let myself take a full day off up to that point ('must focus!'). That day, however, I took myself out to morning tea off Piccadilly, went to Hyde Park, took a long walk and ended by the ponds, watching a mother duck and her fledglings doing their free range thing. I came back with more ideas and inspiration than I'd had in a month.

I still take this approach today: one blog post might start its life while I am lying on the couch, and then get finished when I'm sitting in the park; when I create a product I'll ask, 'Where do I need to be to do this justice?' and I'll move, say, to a café or wherever I know I'll get the best results at that moment. You can get into this practice even before quitting your job. Today, segment your home into regions. One for research, one for creativity, one for 'doing the work' and the rest for whatever you

▶

choose. If you only have a single room, no problem: decide one corner is for creating and one for planning.

Next look at your inputs. Are you surrounding yourself by inspiring people who make you feel your dream is possible? It is almost impossible to make a change if you only hear the words of people who don't think it's possible! Even if you don't know any free rangers right now, you can make sure you are reading the right books, browsing free range friendly websites, immersing yourself in the perspective of those who think like this.

The more you surround yourself with the words and thoughts of people who are doing what you want to do, the more you'll start to believe that this is simple: that 'everyone' does it, and it's not such a big leap after all. We humans tend to believe what is in front of our eyes and that means if you spend time with a certain type of person you start to believe that their type of life is the norm, and your actions reflect that. So average out the income of the six people you spend the most time with, and you'll get a figure somewhere near your own income. Average out the self-belief of the people around you, and you'll start to understand why your own self-belief set-point is where it is. You get out what you put in, so make sure what you're putting in is benefiting you.

Not sure where to find other free range fledglings? Check out the fabulous community on the Free Range Humans Facebook page: **www.facebook.com/freerangehumans**

31 HOW TO LIVE AND WORK ANYWHERE

'Instead of wondering when your next vacation is, maybe you should set up a life you don't need to escape from.' *Seth Godin*

This book opened with a travel story. And I know that while not everyone is into globetrotting, for many people part of the appeal of free ranging is the potential to travel more, or to simply live and work anywhere you choose. Indeed this was part of my dream when I was back in a job.

Back then, I didn't know anyone who lived the sort of lifestyle I had in mind and I had no idea how to make it happen. However, it turns out that life is much more accessible than I thought. Here's how I did it (and how you can too).

Hello from Thailand!

For the past month I've been running my business out of Phuket... in the sunshine of a little hideaway complete with waterfall and palm trees.

This is not a holiday... it's not a one-off short break before coming back to 'reality'. This is me running my regular life, just in a different place... and with more roosters.

You know the best thing? Unless I told you I was in a hammock right now, then you'd never know. If you were a client you'd still work with me as usual. You'd still get my courses, get replies, and I'd still be building and growing my business just the same as if I was sitting 200 metres from wherever you're reading this from right now. There's no difference to my business (the client experience or bottom line) if I'm in London or Luang Prabang.

Is it 'realistic' to run a business from the other side of the world? The naysayers love to say it's a crazy dream that just can't happen. So let's talk about reality for a moment:

★ The 'reality' is that so long as I have a good wireless Internet connection and my teeny little laptop I can run my business from anywhere I choose (and so can you).

★ The 'reality' is that, while I was exploring South-East Asia with my business in my backpack, my business earned as much as (and a bit more) than back in London.

★ The 'reality' is that full-time travel does not have to be expensive. In fact, it will probably be cheaper than the life you are living today. It's natural to assume that travel costs are going to be as high as that prized annual vacation from the office. But when you are in one place for a while, you can get a great deal on accommodation, you learn where to buy food as the locals do and you can end up spending far less than if you stayed at home. This is the hidden side of location independence: taking advantage of currency differences in order to make your income go much further.

Sounding more realistic yet? I hope so, because you are not alone. The 'reality' is that more and more cubicle-cage refugees are choosing this lifestyle. The location-independent movement is filled with people from all walks of life:

Jon and Lea Woodward have travelled the world for five years, starting in Panama, and kept going for several years after the arrival of their first child. Lea, a former management consultant, explains: 'It's not just about being nomadic and travelling the world to exotic destinations. It's about the freedom to choose the kind of lifestyle that works for you. From wherever you choose to be.' Jon is an illustrator and Lea is an online entrepreneur with many different websites.[17]

Nora Dunn, author of the Professional Hobo blog, explains that in her old life, 'I was in a suit, a successful financial planner appearing on TV. Six months later I was walking through chicken shit and milking goats in Hawaii. I loved it.' Nora travels the world full-time almost for free, volunteering and housesitting for accommodation year round.[18]

As for me, I have travelled both as a single and a couple, with travel buddies and alone, running my business from the UK, Bali, Thailand, USA, Central America, Italy, Hong Kong, Cambodia, Laos, Malaysia, and back where I grew up on the east cost of Australia. As a bit of a 'nester' I like to rent my own space, and stay for at least a month at a time, sometimes three to six months.

This is just a snapshot. There are hundreds more playing out their adventures, their way. Want to join us?

Choose your own adventure

This is how a location-independent lifestyle looks: *any way you choose*. Some travellers keep a home back in their native country, and rent it out while they are on the road. Others don't own a home at all. Some travellers like to hop from destination to destination. Other travellers hunker down for six months or longer and get to know the people and places intimately.

Your free range lifestyle is exactly what you make of it.

TIP   **Two ways to make any business location-independent**

You don't need to teach English overseas, invest in and run a B&B, or win the lottery in order to have the freedom to live and work anywhere. Here are two simple ways to make yourself location-independent:

Choose a naturally portable business

A location-independent business is usually run online and is quite often a mixture of selling services (consulting, coaching, web design, etc) or virtual products (e-books, guides or membership of groups). It is sometimes supplemented with the sale of advertising space or affiliate products. In other words, it is a classic free range business as outlined in Chapter 11.

The main difference is that the way you deliver services is remote rather than face-to-face.

▶

◀

Change a location-dependent business

If your business is of the type that is conventionally tied to one location, simply ask: how can I take this idea and make it work virtually?

For example, when I decided to make my business location-independent, people said it wasn't possible for the sort of work I did. There were a few strands of my businesses that were doing well but which kept me tied to one place. Plus, most of my clients insisted on face-to-face consulting. I was told I simply couldn't make this work virtually.

Of course, as a Free Range Human I just did it anyway. I considered what was most important to me and made changes so I could travel. I dumped the parts of my business that were tying me down (saying *no* to some rather nice income), and consolidated the rest of the work into groups run entirely on the phone and online using the resources outlined in the £100 starter pack in Chapter 13.

I promoted the benefits of being able to join my groups from anywhere in the world. The result was that I ended up with a new, fabulous, diverse group of clients from all around the world, who would never have found me or each other had I remained a 'one location only' business. Since then, my business has only grown.

Focus on the advantages

While there might be people lining up to tell you the disadvantages of being remote, you can actually turn this new way of working into an advantage for you and your customers.

One advantage is increased reach. Sure, you say 'no' to a few locals who want to see you in the flesh, but you potentially gain much more than that. Right now, your current potential customer base is probably restricted to whoever can conveniently get to your location. How many more customers could you expect if you expanded that to include the next town? And the next city? Then, what if your reach went as far as the whole world? Big businesses spend millions 'going global' to reach more people; as a Free Range Human you can go global from day one.

Another advantage is convenience for your customers. By moving to telephone or online interactions, there is no need for a client to trek from their office to see you face-to-face. Instead of apologizing for not being there in person, make it clear that they will always be able to talk to you from the privacy and comfort of their home.

Articulate the advantages for your niche: for example if you're a personal stylist, can you launch as a virtual stylist for busy people who don't have time to meet anyone face-to-face? You could integrate photos, Skype sessions, online shopping and other creative bits and bobs to make your virtual-styling offering an asset rather than a compromise.

MINI CASE STUDY

As a book editor it might seem strange that I spend most of my time on the other side of the world from most of my clients. I am in Australia while they are in the USA and UK. However, I have turned this into an advantage: I edit and return chapters in time for when those authors wake up the next morning, which speeds up the process!

Robert Watson, Newcastle, Australia

Finally, if you're really scared that your people will be put off by you being away, try it out for a month without telling anyone. You can easily be 'a London-based nutritionist offering telephone consultations'... so what if you happen to be in South America at the time of a call? So long as you're delivering what you promised, at the quality you promised, then no one need notice unless you want them to.

Wait, what about the children?

On my travels I have met plenty of free range families with kids of all ages. Again and again I've been blown away by how intelligent and advanced 'free range kids' tend to be.

A mum who has lived this life for years is Jeanne of **http://www.soultravelers3.com**; she travels the world with her husband and their 11-year-old daughter and has done so since their daughter was 5. Jeanne says, 'Raising our daughter as a fluent trilingual world citizen was one of our main motivations for this lifestyle... today, one can live and school anywhere in the world and all you need is a laptop.'

They homeschool their daughter and, as a result, she has become fluent in Spanish and Mandarin Chinese, as well as a voracious reader, years ahead of age peers in academic learning. She even takes piano lessons in Spain – via Skype with a teacher in Chicago.

As for developing friendships, their advice is to immerse with the locals and return regularly. Over winter, they spend five months in one place and have returned to one village and school for four winters consecutively, giving her time to connect with regular friends. For the resources Jeanne's family uses for schooling see this article: **http://frh.me/longtermfamilytravel**

MINI CASE STUDY

Travelling with a baby on the road is no more difficult than having a baby in general. He was very portable at six months, so we'd just pick him up and go. Travelling with a child is like a bridge to another culture. As a regular traveller you're labelled as a tourist, but as a couple with a small child people are more likely to stop and have meaningful interactions. We spent several months in South America and people would run across the road to greet us going 'oh your baby is so beautiful' and would go out of their way to ensure we were okay.

Christine Gilbert, **www.almostfearless.com**

TIP   Packing list: essentials to pack (and download)

My backpack contains the following 'work' items:

1 laptop;

2 smartphone (which doubles as my camera and video recorder);

3 backup drive, just to be safe.

That's really all the physical items you need in luggage in order to run your business.

Before leaving make sure you set up the following on your laptop:

★ Google docs – this is a free service that lets you work on the same document with people on the other side of the world and see changes come up live as you make them. Amazing for collaborations.

★ A Cloud backup to save your files online as well, in case your bag disappears. I use Dropbox (it also has an app that makes your Dropbox files available on your smartphone as well).

★ Skype to make phone calls for low cost and to give you a virtual number for friends and family to call (as explained in Chapter 13).

These resources and more are listed here:
http://frh.me/topresources

Travel checklist

Decided you want to do it? Brilliant! Here are the basics to get yourself homed, insured and online:

Internet

Find cafés or accommodation with wifi Internet (or buy a data stick in the country). Internet is available in most places in the world – I found wireless Internet in Laos in a village that barely had hot water. But do check in advance.

Travel insurance

If you will be out of the country for more than 60 days it is possible that normal travel insurance will not cover you. Most free rangers I know use World Nomads **http://frh.me/worldnomadinsurance**

Accommodation

Most of the best deals on accommodation are to be found on the ground – a rule of thumb is to check on travel forums about how packed a place is. If it's likely to be crowded, book your accommodation in advance. If it's not crowded, find somewhere for the first few days – or weeks – and then source your medium-term home when on the ground.

Some basic websites for quickly getting an idea of area are **www.wikitravel.org** (worldwide) and **www.travelfish.org** (South-East Asia) and specific travel blogs for different regions.

My regular website for pre-booking is Airbnb. People rent out their rooms or whole apartments and it is very safe. I've used them dozens of times and am a big fan (partly because of the handy smartphone app for finding places on the road!). Airbnb is also a safe way of renting out your place when you travel and this can more than pay your rent/mortgage if you want to keep a home base. **http://frh.me/travelairbnb**

If you're feeling intrepid you can also do what some people, including Joan Bell (a 60-year-old free ranger) and my colleague Selina Barker, have each done and get a campervan to travel and work from for six months or longer!

Stay for free

Nora Dunn (your friendly professional hobo) spent precisely $178 on her accommodation in 2011. Total. The rest she found for free in various ways, including volunteering and housesitting. Nora says:

In Grenada I housesat a gorgeous villa, owned by a UK couple who split their time between countries and needed someone to take care of the place when they're away. With beautiful hikes everywhere, and use of vehicles, all I had to do was run occasional errands and be company for the dog. I stayed there for three months and I'm going back in March for more. A beautiful free place in the Caribbean – how could you go wrong?

To find housesitting opportunities register for websites such as **www.housecarers.com** and **www.caretaker.org**. These resources do charge a fee but you more than make it back in one housesitting gig.

'Where should I go first?'

It's completely up to you! Generally, make sure there is good Internet and access to whatever facilities you want. Unless you are keen to hop around, choose somewhere to stick with for a month at the minimum, as that's how long it takes to start to get familiar with a new home.

Current popular location-independent destinations include Thailand (Bangkok, Chiang Mai and the Southern islands), Argentina (Buenos Aires), the southern European countryside (Italy, Spain, France), the Greek Islands and Bali.

MINI CASE STUDY

I was on track to becoming vice president of a successful company. Only problem was I was dreadfully unhappy about it. Every morning I'd get up and commute from my flat in Camden (London) and everything looked grey. My job sucked and I couldn't stand the politics, but I had no idea what to do about it.

On a free range course I was set a six-week challenge to change something about my life. I took it on: I booked a short vacation, got a flight to Australia and lined up networking meetings to find myself a contract over there. Long story short, by the end of the six-week challenge I had resigned, and within months all my worldly possessions and I were on a one-way flight to Sydney.

That's where I'm living now, looking over the blue harbour waters every day. Since then I have run my first triathalon, created a work lifestyle I love, and for the first time ever I know that I can make anything happen. Oh, and I met Richard Branson on that first flight to Australia but that's another story. That's just the sort of thing that happens when you take on free range challenges!

Dave Brown, Sydney, Australia

32 HOW TO QUIT YOUR JOB: 10 STEPS TO FREEDOM

> 'The ability to invent a desired future is directly dependent upon the willingness to break with the past.' *Robert J Kriegel*

When you're thinking of quitting your job, people might ask: 'how can you throw away everything you have worked for?'

I have a different question for those people: 'how can you throw away your *life*?' That you invested time and money in a direction that no longer suits you is not a reason to go further in that wrong direction. This is your one life. *Don't throw it away.*

I know you've read this far for a reason. Something chimed with you. You're starting to see possibilities, dream big. The worst thing you could do is put this book back on the shelf and think 'nice dream, maybe one day...'

This is it, honey. This, right here, is your chance for something more. You don't have to leap tomorrow but you do have to commit, to yourself, that you are going to make a change. To help you do that, here are 10 steps for taking the ideas in this book and creating your freedom... starting today:

1. Go free range from today

From today think of yourself as a Free Range Human with one client: your employer. From now on, you work with this 'client' because it is part of your own plans, a source of funding to get where you want to go.

So, get practice at acting like a Free Range Human while in your job. In Chapter 6, I set you a free range action to create a taste of your dream free-range life, in your regular work day. For example, while in my job, I convinced my boss to let me go to a café for a few hours at a time to work on projects; someone else got their taste of freedom simply by varying the route to work. Did you do that exercise? If not, go and do it now.

Another version is to revise how you allow your current work (your job) to eat into your real career (your free range plans). For example, have you let work creep into your life so that you never leave the office anywhere near on time? Is your job leaving you feeling overwhelmed even after you shut down and get home in the evening? If so, here's your challenge: this week, say 'no' to a request that is a step too far. Say 'no' politely, but firmly. Don't get upset or defensive, just hold your ground and articulate that, for example, your current workload won't allow you to take on that extra task and still deliver quality. If people are used to you saying 'yes' they will probably try to convince you to do it anyway, so you may need to repeat that clear 'no' a few times until it sinks in.

One of my friends tried this. Because she was usually such a yes-woman, her boss was amazed the first time she said no, but from that moment, up until the day she left, she was treated with more respect. Every time you do one of these actions, you are building up your free range muscle and reminding yourself that even though you might still be in that job, you are not a career-cage victim anymore!

Those are a few ideas to get you started. Now it's your turn. This week, what can you do to act like a Free Range Human and surround yourself with free range inspiration while still in your job? Write it here:

_____

Note: Act at your discretion. If you have a sensitive work environment and know these actions will put your job at risk too early, adapt them so they work for you.

2. Clarify what you need

Make sure that every day you stay is a day that contributes to your exit. Be that in terms of improved finances, clearer ideas, or your free range business built up 'on the side' before you quit. To ensure you are staying for the right reasons, clarify your quitting criteria:

★ Where do you want to be with your business when you leave your job? (For instance, I will quit as soon as I have three clients on the books.)

_____

★ How can you make sure this happens? (ie How will you find time to apply the strategies in this book or learn more?)

_____

★ Is there anything you need help with before moving forward? Where will you go to find that?

_____

★ How many months of reserve money would you need in order to feel comfortable leaving your job? (Three months' worth?) Write down the exact figure you want in the bank before you quit:

_____

★ How long will it take you to build up to that amount? Will you need to do something differently to reach that amount? (Or, do you already have the amount you need?)

_____

Now, if you're going to need to save more to reach that figure, make sure it happens by doing this: log in to your bank account and set up a standing order to automatically transfer a set amount to a separate account each payday. This separate bank account is your Free Range Freedom Fund.

Note: it is essential you set this up as an automatic transfer rather than doing it manually. You'll be surprised how quickly your fund will build up when you don't have a chance to spend the money in the first place!

★ Identify what else you need to sort out before you go (eg: US-based readers would include 'health insurance' on this list, and others might include 'remortgage'.)

_____

As you complete each of these milestones come back here and tick them off. You're on your way!

3. Give yourself an escape clause

The best-laid plans go awry. In my last job, I had been building up my business on the side of a demanding full-time job. I created a perfect escape plan (well, perfect on paper). I'd been running my prototype projects (in between 60-hour work weeks), had a brand name and a niche and, even better, I'd finally convinced my boss to let me go part-time! The perfect segue into free range life.

But it never happened. The week before I was set to go part-time, the job finally got all too much and I handed in my resignation there and then. Before I was fully ready. In the middle of a recession too. But I was beyond excited. In my notice period, I built that website I had been talking about for so long, started on the Instant Status steps and made Faststart connections so that by the time I landed on day one I was already out there.

Finally free, I went down the portfolio career route and added in the strand of consulting in my old field. Getting those consulting gigs smoothed the way for the first few months – and was great practice! Getting out there full-time meant I built up the business much faster as well.

Bottom line: if you know you might suddenly want out ASAP, consider what else you can do to earn money before your dream free-range business is ready. Write your answer here:

_____

4. Set a date

Looking at the above, how long do you think it will take you to reach your leaving goals? Are you willing to wait for that date? If it's too long to wait, go back and revise what you think you need (it is usually more than possible to start with less).

Then, commit. Mark your leaving date in your calendar, and write it here:

_____

5. Do it

When that date hits, do it.

Danielle La Porte puts this really well: '[if you want to jump] you've got to set a date and you need to honour the date when you get there.... *no matter what*. Because if you pass that *no matter what* date and you haven't seized it, you start to die. You betray yourself, and that's the worst kind of betrayal.'

6. Get ready for a headrush

You're finally free!

Don't underestimate the rush that comes when you're out of the career cage, away from 'those people', and the daily commute. The liberation is wonderful. You can do anything, be anywhere! You wake up later... no need to rush out the door. You walk to your local park at 2 pm and have coffee with that friend who works odd hours... and all the while no one is checking up on you. It feels deliciously naughty: is this *allowed*?

You get out your computer and work on your business long into the night because you're so excited. There's nowhere to be the next day so you can do what you like! This is wonderful, you can't believe you didn't do it earlier.

And then... fear strikes. Bam.

Welcome to the slump. Every free ranger goes through this. It has nothing to do with how much money you've saved or how well you are doing – and everything to do with the realization that, for the first time ever, you're in charge of your life. You start to wonder if you're crazy for imagining you can do this. At least once you will browse the job ads. Some people call this a reason to quit. I call it your first month.

At least once you will be tempted by an offer of work that would take you off the path that feels right. You might even take it for a while, and that's fine. But *don't get into a habit of saying 'yes' out of fear*. Every free ranger has a story of the moment they said 'no' to the easy option – and often that was their turning point.

If you want an amazing life you've got to give up the 'good enough' to get the great. That's when things really change.

7. Gather your support crew

When you quit your job, odds are you won't know many free rangers. When I quit, I had precisely two friends who didn't work regular hours (and neither of them had their own businesses). Now, that's turned around and many of my friends can be found roaming cubicle-free in the 9–5.

Get out there and connect with people. Use the ideas in this book to go to those events, contact those people, build-up relationships. Above all, realize that you are human, and you will benefit from having people 'on your side'. As I show in this video, this is the part most career-cage escape stories leave out: **http://frh.me/ youneedtoknowvideo**

Watch that and then, go get that support crew in place.

8. Learn

> *It's probably not a coincidence that most successful self-bossers are also passionate lifelong learners. They know that learning is an investment, not an expense.* Barbara Winter

When I started out I got to know two other people launching in the same field at the same time. Their ventures never really took off, yet mine did. I don't think for one second that I was better than them. But I do remember, time and time again, that I'd make the choice to attend that seminar, join that course, read that blog, and lap up the techniques and learnings that came my way. On each course I would get at least one insight that got me excited, then I'd go home and apply it straight away... and it would quickly pay for itself.

The other two, sadly, never came with me. They said they wanted to wait until they were 'more established' to invest in themselves. I suspect that's why they never really got established. When you go free range, you are your business. Investment in yourself and your education is the one thing that will reap rewards over and over.

9. Do

Learning without action won't get you anywhere. When you learn something new don't say 'great idea, I should really write that down', say 'I'm scheduling it into the diary to do ASAP'.

Every day ask yourself 'what are the next three things I need to know before I can take the next step?' Learn those three things *and then go do them.*

10. Take the reins

You're in charge now. What do you want to do? It's important you get in the habit of listening to yourself, and stopping to notice those 'oh yeah!' moments. So, you get to choose Step 10. What three things in this book have made the biggest impact on you? How will you use those insights in your life from now on?

What stood out for me	What I am going to do about it

Notes

1 Fried, J and Heinemeier Hansson, D (2009) *ReWork*, Crown Business, New York
2 *What Happened To That Fail: 8 June 2010*, NY Tech Meetup, http://livestre.am/brKR
3 Read more about Terri and her work at her website http://www.inspiredlivelihood.com
4 As a result of her new niche, Grace was offered the chance to write a book: "21 Ways to Manage the Stuff That Sucks Up All Your Time"
5 Seth Godin, *Can't Top This*, Seth's Blog, November 2009 http://sethgodin.typepad.com/seths_blog/2009/11/cant-top-this.html
6 See Phil's work at www.phillipvn.com
7 See Connie's words and work at http://www.dirtyfootprints-studio.com
8 *Don't get put off by feeling you have to approach the world's biggest bloggers like in these examples. Benny had got himself off the ground*

before making these connections with these people, and he did that by guesting on more accessible blogs – you can do this too.

9 http://sethgodin.typepad.com/seths_blog/2007/06/selling-adverti.html

10 *How Spanx Became A Billion Dollar Business Without Advertising,* *Forbes,* 3 December 2012, http://www.forbes.com/sites/clareoconnor/ 2012/03/12/how-spanx-became-a-billion-dollar-business-without-advertising/

11 To be clear, networking meetings have their place – in fact you may well pick up your first pieces of work in that setting should you so choose. These events are also a great space to get known and build relationships with other people in your field. However, my point is that, unless you truly love that sort of event, this is not the best *primary* source of clients for free rangers, simply because you have to go out and pitch to individuals rather than having groups of people constantly coming to *you*. A reliable income shouldn't depend on you showing up to a meeting.

12 Gottman, J M (1994) *What Predicts Divorce: The Relationship Between Marital Processes and Marital Outcomes,* Lawrence Erlbaum, New York

13 See Hattie's latest project at www.peoplelikeus.me.uk

14 MacLeod, Hugh, 2011, *Evil Plans: Escape the rat race and start doing something you love,* Marshall Cavendish International, Singapore

15 Pallota, D, I Don't Understand What Anyone Is Saying Anymore, *Harvard Business Review* (Blog Network), 5 December 2011, http://blogs.hbr.org/pallotta/2011/12/i-dont-understand-what-anyone. html

16 Orwell, George, *Essays,* Penguin Classics, New edition (2000)

17 See more about Lea at http://www.leawoodward.com

18 See Nora at www.theprofessionalhobo.com

EPILOGUE YOU'RE NOT BUILDING A BUSINESS, YOU'RE CREATING A LIFE

'There is no passion to be found playing small –
in settling for a life that is less than the one you are
capable of living.' *Nelson Mandela*

At the beginning of this book I told you that a few weeks after I left my teens, my Mum died of cancer.

Here is the part I didn't tell you: if you've read even one page of this book then you've heard Mum somewhere in there. She's the real 'free range mum', the secret powerhouse behind this movement.

So, today, I'm stripping back the layers and giving you a full whoosh of Mumness with the five lessons she taught me that form the basis of the free range approach, and that I'd like to leave you with as you start your journey.

1. Be wonderful

Mum was the mum everyone wanted. She loved everyone. Once you walked into the house, she wouldn't let her broken Mauritian-accented English hold her back from letting you know how special you were.

My schoolfriend Claire called her Smiley, because she was:

Claire: Ah, Smiley. I miss her. She would be so proud of you, I know. I miss those crepes, and the pain d'epice, and the way she pronounced 'lollipop', the way she would constantly feed me and made me feel like I was treasured.

Mum expressed love through hugs and listening – deeply listening, not just thinking of what she would say next. That's rare.

Mostly, she cared through food. My friends came over after school, and she would make the thinnest crepes served with Nutella, or lemon and sugar. The bottom slightly browned, the middle yellow and chewy, rolled up just right. Hungry or not, come into her house and you would leave well-fed. There was always someone at the kitchen table sharing a cup of tea in her flower-patterned cups.

She assumed the world was a good place, believed people were nice at heart, and did her part to make that a reality.

Free range lesson: care. Genuinely care. Don't assume the world is out to get you – it's not, you know. Holding back is not helping anyone; be wonderful.

2. Learning is better than receiving

Mum loved kids and was passionate about education – when she was younger she started up the first preschool for disadvantaged kids in Mauritius (which grew to five schools around the country).

At the age of 3 Mum took my education into her own hands and taught me how to read. By 3½ I was reading fluently (there's a tape somewhere to prove it!). By 5, I was a speed-reader with a reading age of 10 – thanks to Mum. I've had my nose in a book (or a Kindle) ever since.

But get this: *Mum never read a book out loud to me.* She knew the gift was not in hearing the stories but in showing me how to read and write them myself.

Free range lesson: learn how to do it for yourself – that's the ultimate freedom. Education is the best investment, period.

3. Be your own boss

Mum never told me to do my homework.

Don't get me wrong, she made it clear that I *would* do well in school; failure was never even an option. But she didn't tell me to do my homework and she certainly never did it for me. Turns out that was a pretty smart move. Never having associated schoolwork with being 'told what to do', I didn't have the usual school-kid resistance to doing the work; after all, who would I be rebelling against? More to the point, it meant that I grew up a total nerd (thanks, Mum).

One day, Mum thought she should be more like the other parents, so she told me to do my homework as soon as I got home. I kicked up a stink and that was the first time I didn't do it. She never asked again.

At that point it should have been clear I would be a crappy employee.

Now, it's blindingly obvious that without knowing it, Mum taught me to be an entrepreneur (do well because you want to). But the school system told me to be an employee (do things because you're told to, stay out of trouble because we say so, toe the line).

Free range lesson: be your own boss. It's not enough to lose your boss, you have to learn how to take on that role, starting now.

4. Inhabit your quirks

Mum grew up speaking French – one of a colonial Mauritian family of nine. Despite marrying my firmly monolingual English father, and living most of her life in Anglophone countries, she never quite 'got' the English language.

Heavily accented English with smatterings of French made for an excruciatingly embarrassing Mum for a young kid who just wanted to fit in in Australia! Luckily, Mum never paid attention to my childish wish to be more 'normal'. Mum created her own unique way of speaking and it was part of her charm and accessibility. You can't be scared of someone who says *loolipoop*.

Free range lesson: embrace your quirks. Trying to be someone else will only make you unhappy. What if you believed that those characteristics that the beige army (or an 8-year-old kid) say are 'too weird' are the very things that deserve to be treasured?

5. You'll win! Of course you will (now it's time for you to believe that)

From when I was a young age, Mum and I would play board games together.

When I was really young she let me win every time, so I grew up with the assumption I could never lose. Mum said that when I got older, she stopped letting me win and started playing me properly.

Thing was, by that time, because I never had an experience of losing I just kept on winning – my 8-year-old brain didn't understand how someone could possibly be better than me, so I just didn't let that be the case.

This is going to sound odd, and for that reason I don't say it often, but I want to tell you the truth: to this day I *literally don't understand* why you would not think you're good enough.

★ Why on earth *should* anyone be better than you?

★ Why should someone – not so different to you – be able to create what you can't?

★ Tell me again: do you have one good reason why anyone should be more entitled to this than you?

The last question is so confusing to me that my mind explodes at the thought (told you it was a weird one!). Someone once told me that I had a massive sense of entitlement – and I don't think it was meant as a compliment. But I took it as one (well, of course I did, what with a massive sense of entitlement and all).

Want to know why it's a compliment?

Without a sense of entitlement you don't have an inkling of what you deserve. In fact, you probably don't think you deserve anything more than what you have. *And there's little chance you'll go for something you don't believe you deserve.* You may dabble and toy with the idea but if you don't believe – truly believe – that you deserve this, then nothing anyone says will count.

Mum gave me that confidence and belief to create my best life. As I write this book and the free range blog that's what I'm trying to give you too.

I spend a lot of time joking and writing sharp pithy messages but I just want to share something with you today: I pour my heart and soul into this work – sometimes posts flow out in 10 minutes, other times I spend a day writing and throw away 10 different drafts before one hits your inbox. Often I get emails saying 'that part of your message made me cry'. It's okay, I was probably welled up with tears at that line too. *Despite that, I know Mum would have done a better job at this, and I guess I'm just doing my best to do what she would have done for you if she could have.*

As I write to you, it's not just me. It's the care and love I got from Mum, coming through, spilling out across the world, and landing in its rightful home: with *you.*

I wish she was here to tell you that you can create your own life. I wish she could show you you're as special as I know you are. You'd have got served up perfect crepes in the process.

While the naysayers are lining up to point out the flaws in your dreams, I know you can do this. I believe in you. And Mum would have too.

Now go out there and make us proud.

Be a Free Range Human and commit to finding another way of doing things.

Be the person who does it differently; be the example you're looking for.

Then, in a year or so when people look at what you have, they'll ask: 'How on Earth did she/he do that? I wish I was as lucky as them.' But you'll know it wasn't luck.

You're not building a business; you're creating a life, and that takes guts.

Go for it, tiger.

Stay in touch! Keep up with the free range tribe, get messages of support and fresh free range ideas every week straight to your in box. Get them right here: **http://frh.me/stayintheloop**

Go straight there by scanning the QR code with your smartphone or tablet.

INDEX

CPSIA information can be obtained at www.ICGtesting.com
Printed in the USA
BVOW06s1153300715

411135BV00008B/33/P